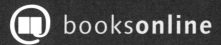 booksonline

Read SAP PRESS online also

With booksonline we offer you online access to leading SAP experts' knowledge. Whether you use it as a beneficial supplement or as an alternative to the printed book – with booksonline you can:

- Access any book at any time
- Quickly look up and find what you need
- Compile your own SAP library

Your advantage as the reader of this book

Register your book on our website and obtain an exclusive and free test access to its online version. You're convinced you like the online book? Then you can purchase it at a preferential price!

And here's how to make use of your advantage

1. Visit www.sap-press.com
2. Click on the link for SAP PRESS booksonline
3. Enter your free trial license key
4. Test-drive your online book with full access for a limited time!

Your personal **license key** for your test access including the preferential offer

6azj-hpdc-eins-5q9k

Transitioning to IFRS in SAP® ERP Financials

 **PRESS**

SAP PRESS is a joint initiative of SAP and Galileo Press. The know-how offered by SAP specialists combined with the expertise of the Galileo Press publishing house offers the reader expert books in the field. SAP PRESS features first-hand information and expert advice, and provides useful skills for professional decision-making.

SAP PRESS offers a variety of books on technical and business related topics for the SAP user. For further information, please visit our website: *www.sap-press.com*.

Subbu Ramakrishnan
Manufacturing Finance with SAP ERP Financials
2009, 584 pp.
978-1-59229-238-7

Naeem Arif, Sheikh Tauseef Muhammad
SAP ERP Financials Configuration and Design
2008, 467 pp.
978-1-59229-136-8

Aylin Korkmaz
Financial Reporting with SAP
2008, 672 pp.
978-1-59229-179-3

Martin Ullmann
Maximizing SAP ERP Financials Accounts Payable
2009, 496 pp.
978-1-59229-198-4

Paul Theobald

Transitioning to IFRS in SAP® ERP Financials

Galileo Press

Bonn • Boston

Galileo Press is named after the Italian physicist, mathematician and philosopher Galileo Galilei (1564–1642). He is known as one of the founders of modern science and an advocate of our contemporary, heliocentric worldview. His words *Eppur se muove* (And yet it moves) have become legendary. The Galileo Press logo depicts Jupiter orbited by the four Galilean moons, which were discovered by Galileo in 1610.

Editor Stephen Solomon
Copyeditor Ruth Saavedra
Cover Design Jill Winitzer
Photo Credit Image Copyright Magic Portfolio. Used under license from Shutterstock.com.
Layout Design Vera Brauner
Production Editor Kelly O'Callaghan
Assistant Production Editor Graham Geary
Typesetting Publishers' Design and Production Services, Inc.
Printed and bound in Canada

ISBN 978-1-59229-319-3

© 2010 by Galileo Press Inc., Boston (MA)

1st Edition 2010

Library of Congress Cataloging-in-Publication Data
Theobald, Paul.
   Transitioning to IFRS in SAP ERP financials / Paul Theobald. — 1st ed.
      p. cm.
   Includes bibliographical references and index.
   ISBN-13: 978-1-59229-319-3 (alk. paper)
   ISBN-10: 1-59229-319-0 (alk. paper)
   1. SAP ERP.   2. Accounting — Computer programs.
3. Accounting — Standards — Computer programs.   4. Financial
statements — Standards — Computer programs.   I. Title.
   HF5679.T44 2010
   657.0285'53 — dc22   2009046021

Contents at a Glance

Contents

Acknowledgments

I would like to thank CMPC for their permission to use their transition to IFRS as a basis for the case study in this book.

I would also like to thank Mr. Eduardo Jure the CEO of CAPE Global Consulting Latin America for his input into this book and help during the CMPC transition to IFRS.

Above all, I would like to thank my wife Courtney and daughter Lauren for motivating and encouraging me to write this book. I could not have done it without your love and support.

Preface

Introduction

This book was written with the aim of providing guidance to companies that are preparing to transition to International Financial Reporting Standards (IFRS) using SAP ERP Financials as the technology platform.

In my view it is certain that companies in the United States (U.S.) will soon follow companies in other countries and report financial statements by IFRS.

The transition to IFRS is a complex project, and it is extremely important that companies start planning the project as soon as possible. There are accounting changes and technology changes that are required, and the earlier these are started, the better. For example, it is recommended that you use the new SAP General Ledger for IFRS, so many companies that presently use the SAP classic General Ledger will need to run a migration project.

> **Note**
>
> Throughout this book, the new SAP General Ledger will be referred to as SAP General Ledger.

My previous book, *Migrate Successfully to the SAP General Ledger*, explained the migration process in detail, and this will be summarized in Chapter 4, SAP Upgrade and General Ledger Migrations. Also, before you can migrate to the SAP General Ledger you must have upgraded to SAP ERP 6.0, so another part of the IFRS transition may include a technical upgrade project.

This book will explain the accounting changes required (with a focus on U.S. companies) and the recommended technical changes to your SAP system.

Transition to IFRS

Many European countries have already made the transition to IFRS. However, other countries such as those in Latin America and Canada are in the process of transitioning to IFRS, and others such as the U.S. plan to in the near future. Other countries have partially transitioned to IFRS, and Chapter 2 will provide a summary of the current situation for all companies worldwide.

The current roadmap for the U.S. was published in 2008 and states that companies will be required to produce IFRS financial statements starting in 2014 and comparative financial statements starting in 2012. However, this is still subject to change and will not be decided by the Securities Exchange Commission (SEC) until 2011. Although there is much speculation that the 2014 date will be pushed back perhaps until 2016, this book will be based on the current roadmap that the SEC has proposed for U.S. companies.

An important point to note is that because the main purpose of this book is using SAP ERP Financials for IFRS, many of the recommendations can and should be started now regardless of whether there is a change in the deadline. For example, many companies using older versions of SAP systems may require an upgrade to SAP ERP and then a migration to SAP General Ledger. These must be two separate projects, and migrations can only occur at a fiscal year end, so even if there is a delay and comparative IFRS statements are not required until 2014, for example, it is wise to start planning your IFRS project now because IFRS is coming soon.

Using SAP Functionality to Assist Transition

There are many ways to use SAP to report IFRS, and this book will describe the recommended approach using SAP General Ledger but will also suggest other alternative solutions using the classic General Ledger.

The new functionality in SAP General Ledger such as parallel ledgers, segment reporting, and document splitting are excellent solutions for IFRS. However, there may be companies that at present are using the classic General Ledger and may not be able to migrate to SAP General Ledger before IFRS is required. This may be due to several reasons such as technical restrictions, budget constraints, and so on, and this book will suggest alternatives to the new functionality such as using parallel accounts instead of parallel ledgers.

As well as changes in SAP functionality in SAP General Ledger to assist the transition to IFRS, there will also be many other changes across several other SAP components, for example, changes in valuations and master data in components such as asset management and materials management.

> **Note**
>
> CAPE Global Consulting is presently running several IFRS transition projects in Latin America. In our experience, most of the valuation and master data changes have been in the asset management component. For example, assets previously valued as single assets may now have to be valued by component parts to meet IFRS requirements. There have also been many changes in the materials management component and specifically the valuation of materials. IFRS does not permit indirect overheads, and the effort required to change these material valuations can be very time consuming.

Intended Audience and Skill Prerequisites

This book is intended for anyone who may be involved in the transition to IFRS. This includes not only those who will be working full time on the IFRS project team, but also those who are involved indirectly, such as other members of the finance department.

Decision makers will gain insight into what is required to run an IFRS project, which will assist in determining the project's time frame, budget, and required staffing.

IFRS project managers will benefit from understanding the project phases required and the methodology and SAP tools available to assist them in running the project.

Members of the finance department and external and internal auditors may mostly benefit from Chapter 2, which provides an overview of the accounting standards and describes the key differences between IFRS and local generally acceptable accounting practices (GAAPs).

Members of the information systems (IS) department may mostly benefit from Chapters 3 and 4, which describe the SAP functionality for IFRS in SAP General Ledger and the technical changes required in SAP systems such as upgrading and general ledger migration.

SAP consultants will also benefit from this guide by increasing their understanding of what has to be changed in SAP systems during an IFRS project. There are technical projects such as upgrading to SAP ERP and migrating to SAP General Ledger, but there are also changes to other functionality and master data. For example, many changes need to be made to asset management configuration and master data.

Knowledge of accounting is useful when reading this book — and knowledge of the SAP General Ledger functionality. However, all of these topics will be explained, and all readers will benefit from learning about the project phases that make up an IFRS project in Chapter 5.

How this Book Is Organized

The main emphasis of this book is on how to transition to IFRS using SAP ERP Financials. However, the book starts by introducing IFRS and describing the current situation worldwide and then explains the main differences between IFRS and local GAAPs (with a focus on U.S. GAAP). A synopsis of each chapter is as follows:

▶ **Chapter 1: Introduction to IFRS**
   This chapter describes the current adoption of IFRS by countries worldwide. Many countries now require IFRS, other countries allow IFRS, and some do not permit IFRS (such as the U.S.). This chapter then describes the current situation in the Americas, concentrating on the U.S.

▶ **Chapter 2: IFRS and Local GAAPs**
   This chapter explains the key accounting differences between IFRS and other local GAAPs for countries that have yet to transition to IFRS such as Canada and the U.S. The chapter starts by providing an overview of the current accounting standards and then describes the key differences between IFRS and local GAAPs for areas such as assets, revenue recognition, and so on.

▶ **Chapter 3: SAP ERP Financials Functionality for IFRS**

This chapter explains how to best use the functionality in SAP ERP Financials for the transition to IFRS. It covers parallel reporting and the two recommended methods, which are parallel ledgers and parallel accounts. It then explains the options for countries that have yet to transition to IFRS and will require either a new installation of SAP ERP or an upgrade followed by a migration project. The chapter then provides an overview of the other new functionality in SAP General Ledger such as segment reporting, document splitting, and foreign currency valuation. There are also sections on consolidations and reporting in the eXtensible Business Reporting Language (XBRL). Finally, the chapter explains the impact of IFRS on other SAP components such as asset management and materials management.

▶ **Chapter 4: SAP Upgrade and General Ledger Migrations**

This chapter discusses the upgrade to SAP ERP and then the migration to SAP General Ledger for companies that are not using SAP ERP and SAP General Ledger already. The chapter then explains the new migration scenarios for companies that are already using SAP General Ledger but need to add new functionality such as parallel ledgers and document splitting in preparation for IFRS.

▶ **Chapter 5: IFRS Transition Project**

This chapter explains the various phases in an IFRS project. It is based on how a typical U.S. company will transition to IFRS and starts with an overview of the current time lines. The chapter then describes the various project phases and activities in an IFRS project starting with a roadmap. This is based on IFRS methodology that was developed by CAPE Global Consulting and has been used in successful IFRS transitions.

▶ **Chapter 6: Case Study**

This chapter describes how a large multinational company transitioned to IFRS. It explains how the accounting and technology changes were implemented and highlights the key lessons learned.

Summary

As explained above, Chapter 1 will introduce IFRS and the current adoption of IFRS worldwide. Chapter 2 is tailored toward accounting and explains the current accounting standards and differences in accounting principles. Chapters 3 and 4 are the main focus of this book and explain how to use SAP ERP Financials for IFRS. Chapter 5 describes the various project phases in an IFRS project, and finally Chapter 6 provides a real-life case study of a company that recently transitioned to IFRS using SAP ERP Financials.

Before discussing the central topics of this book, however, it is important to introduce IFRS and describe the current situation worldwide, and the first chapter will concentrate on this.

International Financial Reporting Standards (IFRS) have been adopted by many countries around the world. At present, over 100 countries either require or allow IFRS, and these include all European countries.

1 Introduction to IFRS

1.1 Introduction

This chapter will discuss the IFRS framework for how standards are published, provide an overview of the current adoption of IFRS worldwide, and examine the current situation for U.S. companies. It is still not clear when the U.S. will move away from U.S. Generally Accepted Accounting Principles (U.S. GAAP), but it seems only a matter of time. By 2011 the U.S. will be the only country not using IFRS.

First, however, we will discuss how IFRS are published.

1.2 IFRS Framework

IFRS are now published by the International Accounting Standards Board (IASB). In 2001 the IASB replaced the International Accounting Standards Committee (IASC) as the organization responsible for setting IFRS. Figure 1.1 shows the structure of the IASB and its relationship to other groups such as the IASC. A monitoring board was set up effective on February 1, 2009, and the main purpose of this board is to appoint and manage the trustees in the IASC.

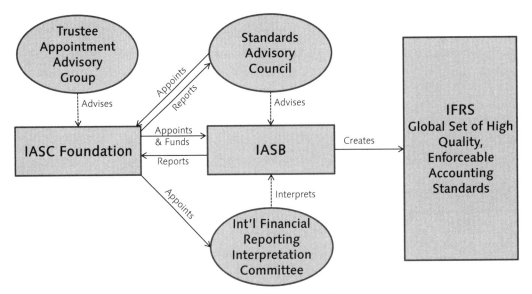

Figure 1.1 Structure of the International Accounting Standards Board

The aim is that the members of the IASB represent a diverse group both geographically and in their professional backgrounds. To ensure a good balance geographically, there are four members from North America, four members from Europe, four members from Asia, one from South America, one from Africa, and two others.

1.3 Accounting Standards

Standards set by the IASC are referred to as International Accounting Standards (IAS), and new standards set by the IAB are referred to as IFRS.

There are 30 IAS and 8 IFRS currently issued, and these are listed with a brief description in Chapter 2.

The assumptions for IFRS are that financial statements are prepared on a:

▶ **Going concern basis**
  The company can continue trading in the foreseeable future.

▶ **Accrual basis**
  Transactions are recognized as they occur, not when they are actually paid.

Financial statements prepared by IFRS must contain the following:

▶ A statement of financial position (balance sheet)

▶ An income statement

▶ A cash flow statement

▶ A statement of changes of equity

▶ Detailed notes on accounting policies

Chapter 2 will also highlight the differences between IFRS and other GAAPs for countries that have yet to transition to IFRS, for example, U.S. GAAP for the U.S. The next section will provide an overview of the countries that now require IFRS and those that have not transitioned.

1.4   Adoption of IFRS by Country

Many countries around the world have already adopted IFRS as the basis for their financial statements. At time of writing, over 110 countries had adopted IFRS, and by 2011 virtually all countries will have transitioned to IFRS except for the U.S. The European Union (EU) mandated IFRS in 2005 for publicly held companies, but most EU countries still do not permit IFRS for private companies.

As an overview, some of the larger countries that already require IFRS include the following:

- Australia and New Zealand
- Belgium, Czech Republic, Denmark, Finland, Germany, Ireland, Norway, Sweden, Switzerland, Netherlands, United Kingdom, France, and Italy
- Bulgaria, Greece, Poland, Portugal, Turkey, Romania
- Pakistan and South Africa
- Chile, Peru, Uruguay, Venezuela

> **Note**
>
> Listed companies in Chile were required to report by IFRS starting on January 1, 2009. CAPE Global Consulting has been the implementation partner for several of the largest IFRS projects in Chile and has its Latin America office based in Santiago, Chile. The case study in Chapter 6 is based on one of our largest IFRS projects in Chile.

Some of the larger countries that at the time of writing have not transitioned to IFRS are:

- Argentina
- Brazil
- Canada
- China
- Columbia
- India
- Japan
- Mexico

▶ Paraguay (IFRS permitted but not required)

▶ Saudi Arabia

▶ Singapore

▶ United States

The next section will discuss the current status for the countries listed above that are not using IFRS yet.

1.5   Current Status for Countries not Using IFRS

This section will examine the countries that have yet to permit IFRS and will provide information about when they are likely to do so. Most, if not all, countries are planning to require IFRS by 2011 except for the U.S., and the current status in the U.S. will be discussed in the most detail below.

▶ **Argentina**
  The recommendation is that listed/public companies will be required to report by IFRS starting on January 1, 2011. However, at the time of writing this has not been officially approved by the Argentinean government.

▶ **Brazil**
  All listed/public companies and financial institutions will be required to report consolidated financial statements by IFRS starting on January 1, 2010. This has been approved by the Brazilian Securities and Exchange Commission. However, the financial statements of individual companies must still be reported by Brazilian GAAP.

▶ **Canada**
  The current status in Canada is that all listed/public companies must report by IFRS starting on January 1, 2011. Foreign companies trading on the Canadian stock exchange are permitted to report by IFRS. Nonlisted companies will continue to report in Canadian GAAP from January 1, 2011, but the plan is for Canadian GAAP to converge with IFRS.

▶ **China**
  There is no official deadline to transition to IFRS, but Chinese Accounting Standards (CAS) have mostly converged with IFRS already. The remaining differences will be eliminated in the future.

▸ **Colombia**

There are no plans for IFRS at time of writing.

▸ **India**

The Institute of Chartered Accountants of India (ICAI) recently announced that IFRS will be required in 2011.

▸ **Japan**

The current status is that IFRS is permitted for listed companies starting in 2009, and the plan is to converge all differences between Japanese GAAP and IFRS by 2011.

▸ **Mexico**

The Mexican Banking and Securities Commission has stated that IFRS will be required for all listed/public companies starting on January 1, 2012.

▸ **Paraguay**

IFRS is permitted but not required.

▸ **Saudi Arabia**

At present, IFRS is only permitted for financial institutions that are regulated by the central bank. There are no plans to transition other companies to IFRS.

▸ **Singapore**

Accounting standards in Singapore are very similar to IFRS. At present, only listed/public companies that are required to report on a foreign exchange in IFRS may report in IFRS.

1.5.1   Current Status for the United States

The current status of IFRS in the U.S. is that the requirement for IFRS has not been finalized. However, on November 14, 2008, the Securities Exchange Commission (SEC) proposed a roadmap for the transition to IFRS for U.S. companies. This road-map is shown in Figure 1.3, below, and although it is not final, it proposes that U.S. companies will be required to file financial statements by IFRS for fiscal years ending after December 14, 2014.

Background

The SEC has played a major role in the move to a common set of accounting standards to be used by all countries around the world. As early as 1988, the SEC began to discuss the development of international accounting standards. In

1997 the SEC commented on the problems for multinational companies having to produce financial statements by different accounting standards to meet local requirements.

Later, in 2002, the SEC supported the Norwalk Agreement between the IASB and the Financial Accounting Standards Board (FASB). Part of this agreement was the long-term aim to establish global accounting standards and to converge U.S. GAAP with IFRS.

In 2006, the SEC chairman endorsed a previously published roadmap that had called for the introduction of high-quality, globally accepted accounting standards.

In November 2007, the SEC permitted foreign companies trading on the U.S. stock exchange to file financial statements prepared under IFRS without having to provide reconciliation to U.S. GAAP. Also, in December 2007, the SEC issued a concept release asking for feedback on allowing IFRS for U.S. public companies.

Figure 1.2 provides an overview of the time period up to and including the current proposed roadmap in 2008.

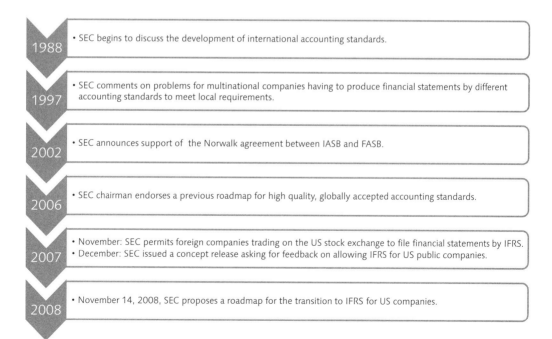

1988
• SEC begins to discuss the development of international accounting standards.

1997
• SEC comments on problems for multinational companies having to produce financial statements by different accounting standards to meet local requirements.

2002
• SEC announces support of the Norwalk agreement between IASB and FASB.

2006
• SEC chairman endorses a previous roadmap for high quality, globally accepted accounting standards.

2007
• November: SEC permits foreign companies trading on the US stock exchange to file financial statements by IFRS.
• December: SEC issued a concept release asking for feedback on allowing IFRS for US public companies.

2008
• November 14, 2008, SEC proposes a roadmap for the transition to IFRS for US companies.

Figure 1.2   SEC Timeline 1988-2008

Proposed SEC Roadmap

As mentioned previously, the proposed roadmap is not final, and the SEC will review the feedback that it has received and whether milestones have been met in 2011. Depending on the feedback that the SEC receives, it may phase in the requirement for IFRS in 2014 depending on market capitalization. For example, the largest companies will be required to report IFRS in 2014, with others following in subsequent years.

The seven milestones that the SEC will review the progress of in 2011 are as follows:

- ▶ The improvement of current specific accounting standards
- ▶ The current funding of the FASB
- ▶ The ability to use XBRL for IFRS
- ▶ The current education and training of U.S. accountants
- ▶ Evaluating the success of U.S. early adopters of IFRS
- ▶ Timing of future rule making by the SEC
- ▶ Determining when to make IFRS required for U.S. companies, such as in 2014 or a possible phased approach

In the roadmap, the SEC proposed that early adopters meeting certain criteria be allowed to elect to file financial statements by IFRS for fiscal years ending on or after December 15, 2009.

Figure 1.3 shows the proposed roadmap as it is today, with the final decision to be made in 2011.

Benefits for IFRS in the U.S.

The main obvious benefit to having companies in all countries reporting by IFRS is that financial statements can easily be compared between companies in different countries. This will help investors, who can then more easily evaluate companies using the same criteria, and it will also help companies consolidate their financial results from their subsidiaries in other countries.

As shown in the previous section, IFRS has or will be adopted in most countries in the world by 2011, and the U.S. will be the only one remaining that has not adopted it.

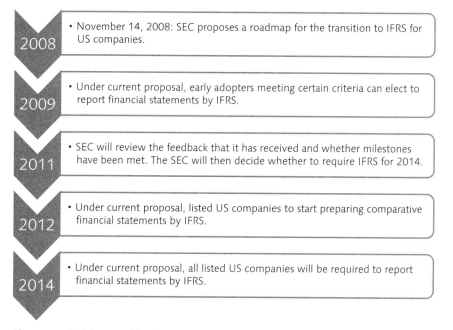

2008	• November 14, 2008: SEC proposes a roadmap for the transition to IFRS for US companies.
2009	• Under current proposal, early adopters meeting certain criteria can elect to report financial statements by IFRS.
2011	• SEC will review the feedback that it has received and whether milestones have been met. The SEC will then decide whether to require IFRS for 2014.
2012	• Under current proposal, listed US companies to start preparing comparative financial statements by IFRS.
2014	• Under current proposal, all listed US companies will be required to report financial statements by IFRS.

Figure 1.3   SEC Proposed Roadmap 2008-2014.

Potential Issues for IFRS in the U.S.

One of the main issues for IFRS in the U.S. is that there are still significant differences between U.S. GAAP and IFRS. There are also supporters of U.S. GAAP who argue that U.S. GAAP actually provides more detail than IFRS. Chapter 2 will explain the significant differences between U.S. GAAP and IFRS. These include some major areas such as:

▸ Revenue recognition

▸ Inventory

▸ Financial assets

- Taxes
- Leases
- Pensions
- Consolidations

The IASB and FASB continue to work on converging the differences between IFRS and U.S. GAAP.

Another issue for IFRS in the U.S. is that the roadmap requires a comparative period starting in 2012, so companies will have to report by two GAAPs for up to three years. This will add to the cost and complexity of the transition to IFRS.

Having a phased approach will help reduce costs because companies that transition later can learn from companies that transitioned earlier. However, having a phased approach also delays the time when all companies are using IFRS and so delays the time when all financial statements can be compared equally.

The previous chairman of the SEC, Christopher Cox, held office between August 3, 2005 and January 20, 2009, and he was a strong supporter of IFRS. During his time in office, the SEC allowed foreign companies listed in the U.S. to report IFRS and produced the roadmap discussed above proposing that IFRS be required for listed U.S. companies in 2014.

Mr. Cox was succeeded by. Mary Schapiro, and it appears that IFRS is less of a priority for her than it was under the previous chairman. During her confirmation hearing she commented on the proposed roadmap, saying, "I will take a big deep breath and look at this entire area again carefully and will not necessarily feel bound by the existing roadmap that's out for comment." However, she has said that she supports global standards, so most observers still feel that IFRS is likely but perhaps with a different timeline.

> **Note**
>
> Many believe that the SEC is evaluating whether the proposed roadmap will put too much pressure on U.S. listed companies at a time of economic crisis. The costs of transitioning to IFRS are substantial, and we believe that although IFRS is inevitable in the U.S., the final roadmap will allow more time for U.S. companies to transition to IFRS. Many of our U.S. customers believe that the SEC will issue a new roadmap in 2011, with a two-year delay and making 2016 the required date for IFRS (2014 for comparative financial statements)
>
> Owing to the economic crisis, the SEC has many issues other than IFRS to consider such as the potential of increased regulation of the financial markets in light of the recent financial scandals.

1.6 Summary

As discussed in this chapter, between now and the final adoption of IFRS, the IASB and FASB will continue to work on the convergence of U.S. GAAP and IFRS. Some observers argue that this will be the way that U.S. companies transition to IFRS rather than having a specific date to adopt IFRS. Many more converging standards are expected before 2011, and one was recently published on consolidations.

This chapter has provided an introduction to IFRS, discussing the IFRS framework and the current adoption of IFRS around the world. Over 12,000 companies in over 100 countries have now adopted IFRS, and soon the U.S. will be the only country that has not. The chapter ended with an explanation of the current status of IFRS in the U.S. and the proposed roadmap that the SEC issued in 2008.

The main purpose of this book, however, is to explain how to transition to IFRS using SAP ERP Financials, and this does not change whether the U.S. adopts IFRS on a specific date or it happens as a convergence of U.S. GAAP and IFRS. Owing to the recent comments by the SEC on IFRS, many U.S. companies are making IFRS less of a priority because they do not know how to proceed and have limited resources owing to the economic crisis.

However, IFRS is coming whether by convergence or by adoption, and we believe that U.S. companies should at least start planning and implementing the changes in SAP systems that IFRS will require. Many of the changes in SAP systems such as upgrading to SAP ERP and migrating to SAP General Ledger require projects that will take 12-24 months to complete. The companies that prepare their SAP systems now for IFRS will benefit in the future. The changes required in SAP systems will be covered in detail in Chapter 3.

The next chapter will focus on the current accounting standards and the current differences between IFRS and local GAAPs, focusing on U.S. GAAP.

This chapter will start by examining the current standards and will then explain the major differences between IFRS and local GAAPs for countries that have yet to transition to IFRS. Special focus will be placed on the differences between IFRS and U.S. GAAP.

2 IFRS and Local GAAPs

2.1 Introduction

Although the main subject of this book is how to transition to IFRS using SAP ERP Financials, it is still useful to have some understanding of the accounting standards so that you can more easily determine the SAP functionality required and the SAP components impacted.

This chapter concentrates on accounting topics because it is important to build the foundation for Chapters 3 and 4, which describe how to meet the challenges posed by these accounting standards with SAP functionality.

The next section will provide a summary of the current accounting standards and, where relevant, the SAP components impacted.

2.2 Summary of IFRS

At present there are eight new accounting standards published by the IASB with the naming convention IFRS xx. The remaining standards were published by the IASC with the naming convention of IAS xx.

The standards in effect at present are shown in Table 2.1.

Standard	Description
IFRS 1	First-time Adoption of International Financial Reporting Standards
IFRS 2	Share-Based Payment
IFRS 3	Business Combinations
IFRS 4	Insurance Contracts
IFRS 5	Non Current Assets Held for Sale and Discontinued Operations
IFRS 6	Exploration for and Evaluation of Mineral Resources
IFRS 7	Financial Instruments: Disclosures
IFRS 8	Operating Segments
IAS 1	Presentation of Financial Statements
IAS 2	Inventories
IAS 7	Cash Flow Statements
IAS 8	Accounting Policies, Changes in Accounting Estimates and Errors
IAS 10	Events After the Balance Sheet Date
IAS 11	Construction Contracts
IAS 12	Income taxes
IAS 16	Property, Plant, and Equipment
IAS 17	Leases
IAS 18	Revenue
IAS 19	Employee Benefits
IAS 20	Accounting for Government Grants and Disclosure of Government Assistance
IAS 21	The Effects of Changes in Foreign Exchange Rates
IAS 23	Borrowing Costs
IAS 24	Related Party Disclosures
IAS 26	Accounting and Reporting by Retirement Benefit Plans
IAS 27	Consolidated Financial Statements
IAS 28	Investments in Associates
IAS 29	Financial Reporting in Hyperinflationary Economies
IAS 31	Interests in Joint Ventures

Table 2.1   Current IFRS Standards

Standard	Description
IAS 32	Financial Instruments
IAS 33	Earnings per Share
IAS 34	Interim Financial Reporting
IAS 36	Impairment of Assets
IAS 37	Provisions, Contingent Liabilities, and Contingent Assets
IAS 38	Intangible Assets
IAS 39	Financial Instruments: Recognition and Measurement
IAS 40	Investment Property
IAS 41	Agriculture

Table 2.1 Current IFRS Standards (Cont.)

The following sections provide an interpretation of the standards in the form of a short overview and description of each current accounting standard. The actual standards are more detailed and contain far more information than could be included in this type of book. For example, full IFRS can have up to 3000 pages with about 3000 disclosure points. Your internal finance team and external auditors must consult the full standards for your IFRS project. The following is just to give the reader a high-level understanding of the standards and the SAP components likely to be impacted.

2.2.1 IFRS 1: First-Time Adoption of IFRS

This standard describes what a company must do when it prepares financial statements using IFRS for the first time.

Key Points

IFRS 1 requires that for the first IFRS financial statements, companies must present an opening balance sheet prepared under IFRS rules. This balance sheet does not need to be reported in the financial statements, but it is the starting point for IFRS.

The standard also requires full disclosure of how the transition to IFRS from the company's previous GAAP such as U.S. GAAP has impacted the financial results.

SAP Components Impacted

This standard impacts all SAP financial reporting components. The main SAP components impacted include SAP General Ledger, consolidation, and reporting and analytic tools.

2.2.2 IFRS 2: Share-Based Payment

This standard prescribes the financial reporting required when a company makes share-based payments.

Key Points

This standard requires that companies recognize all share-based transactions in their financial statements. The standard specifies three types of share-based transactions and how to value each:

1. **Equity Settled**

   When a company receives goods and services as payment for equity of the company, the transaction should be valued at the fair value of the goods and services. When fair value for the goods and services cannot be accurately determined (such as services provided by employees), the transaction must be valued at the fair value of the equity. Fair value of goods and services should be determined as of the date that the goods and services were received.

2. **Cash Settled**

   When a company acquires goods and services and as payment incurs a liability that is based on the value of equity, the transaction should be valued at the fair value of the equity. Fair value of equity should be determined from market prices.

3. **Equity or Cash Settled**

   When a company receives or acquires goods and services and the company or supplier can then determine whether payment is by cash or equity, the transaction should be valued as in types 1 and 2 above.

Under this standard, a company must disclose:

- ► The types of share-based transactions that were incurred during the period
- ► How fair value for goods and services and equity was determined
- ► The total impact of the share-based transactions on the company's income statement

SAP Components Impacted

The main SAP components impacted include SAP General Ledger, human resources, and consolidation.

2.2.3   IFRS 3: Business Combinations

This standard explains the financial reporting that is required for a business combination.

Key Points

This standard states that a business combination occurs when separate companies combine into one reporting entity. In nearly all cases, there is a controlling company that is the acquirer, which must report all assets and liabilities acquired at fair value.

Fair value is defined as the total of the assets and liabilities acquired, equity issued as payment, and costs incurred for the combination.

Goodwill is defined as the acquirer's total payment for the combination less the fair value of the assets and liabilities acquired (including contingent liabilities).

If the goodwill is positive, it must be recognized as an asset and cannot be amortized to the income statement. It must be reexamined yearly for impairment in accordance with IAS 36 Impairment of Assets, which we will explain later. If the goodwill is negative, it must be shown as an expense in the income statement.

Under this standard, a company must disclose:

- ► Any business combinations that happened during the period
- ► Business combinations that took place in previous periods and after the balance sheet date

SAP Components Impacted

The main SAP components impacted include SAP General Ledger, consolidation and reporting and analytics.

2.2.4 IFRS 4: Insurance Contracts

This standard describes the financial reporting required for a company that issues insurance contracts (insurers).

Key Points

This standard requires insurers to follow these rules:

1. There are no provisions for insurance claims that are not in existence and therefore not known about at the financial year end such as catastrophes.

2. Adequacy of insurance liabilities must be tested, and there must also be an impairment test for reinsurance assets.

3. Insurance liabilities must not be offset with reinsurance assets.

Under this standard, a company must disclose:

▸ The amounts pertaining to insurance contracts
▸ The timing and uncertainty of cash flows resulting from the insurance contracts

2.2.5 IFRS 5: Noncurrent Assets Held for Sale and Discontinued Operations

This standard describes the financial reporting required for noncurrent assets held for sale and the disclosure of discontinued operations.

Key Points

This standard requires noncurrent assets to be valued at the lower of carrying amount and fair value less costs to sell. The standard introduces the term *held for sale* for assets that are highly likely to be sold (the assets must be available immediately for sale). There is also a new term, *disposal group,* for a group of assets that will be disposed of in a single transaction.

Assets that fall under this new term *held for sale* must be disclosed separately on the balance sheet.

A discontinued operation is defined as a component of an entity that has either been disposed of or is being held for sale. To be classified as a component of an entity, the component must be one of the following:

- A separate major line of business or geographical area of operation
- A part of a single coordinated plan to dispose of a separate major line of business or geographical area of operation
- A subsidiary acquired specifically for resale

The results of discontinued operations must be disclosed separately in the income statement. Therefore, the income statement must be divided into continuing and discontinued operations.

SAP Components Impacted

The main SAP components impacted may include SAP General Ledger, asset management, internal orders, project systems, consolidation and reporting and analytics.

2.2.6   IFRS 6: Exploration for and Evaluation of Mineral Resources

This standard describes the financial reporting required for the exploration and evaluation of mineral resources.

Key Points

This standard is concerned with the costs an entity incurs for the exploration and evaluation of mineral resources before the technical feasibility and commercial viability of extraction is known. Provided that they meet the requirements in IAS 8, the standard specifies that a company can continue to use its existing accounting policies. However, a company must perform an impairment test when the carrying amount of assets related to the exploration and evaluation exceed their recoverable amount.

Under this standard, a company must disclose and explain the amounts related to exploration and evaluation of mineral resources.

2.2.7 IFRS 7: Financial Instruments: Disclosures

This standard complements IAS 32, Financial Instruments: Presentation, and IAS 39, Financial Instruments: Recognition and Measurement. It requires disclosure of financial instruments so that users of financial statements can understand the significance and risks of financial instruments to the company's overall financial position.

Key Points

Under this standard the disclosures required are as follows:

▶ Significance of financial instruments to the company's financial position and performance. Financial instruments include accounts receivable, accounts payable, derivatives, and so on.

▶ Risks that the company is exposed to from the financial instruments. This disclosure must include information on how the risks will be managed.

SAP Components Impacted

The main SAP components impacted may include SAP General Ledger, accounts receivable, accounts payable, treasury, consolidation and reporting and analytics.

2.2.8 IFRS 8: Operating Segments

This standard requires companies to disclose financial information on their operating segments.

Key Points

This standard replaces IAS 14, Segment Reporting, and is a result of work between the FASB and IASB to reduce the differences between IFRS and U.S. GAAP.

An operating segment is defined as a component of a company that meets the following criteria:

- ▶ Management of the company uses the results of the component to make decisions about the company.
- ▶ Separate financial information is available.
- ▶ The component of the company engages in business activities.

The standard defines criteria for when disclosure of an operating segment is required, as follows:

- ▶ The assets of the operating segment exceed 10% of the company's total assets.
- ▶ The revenue of the operating segment exceeds 10% of the company's total revenue.
- ▶ The profit or loss of the operating segment exceeds 10% of the company's total profit or loss.

The standard also states that 75% of a company's revenue must be reported by operating segment and that if this is not the case, additional segments must be reported on even if they do not meet the 10% rule.

In addition, if revenues for a major external customer exceed 10% of the company's total revenue, the customer's revenue must be split by operating segment.

The disclosure for operating segments must include:

- ▶ General information about the segment
- ▶ Financial results of the segment

Note

Segment reporting is a functionality of SAP General Ledger and was not available in the Classic general ledger. Segments can be defined and automatically derived from profit centers, and using segments with document splitting is the perfect solution for IFRS 8 because full balance sheets and income statements can easily be obtained by operating segment. We will explain this in detail in Chapter 3.

SAP Components Impacted

Components impacted include SAP General Ledger, profit center accounting, consolidation and reporting and analytics.

2.2.9 IAS 1: Presentation of Financial Statements

This standard describes how financial statements must be presented to comply with IFRS.

Key Points

Under this standard, for financial statements to be complete they must contain the following:

▸ **Statement of financial position**
Assets and liabilities must be classified as current or noncurrent unless presentation in order of liquidity would provide better understanding.

▸ **Statement of comprehensive income for the period**
This must include all income and expense items related to nonowner changes in equity.

▸ **Cash flow statement**
All cash flows for the period must be presented.

▸ **Statement of changes in equity**
This must show changes in owners' equity, and there must be full reconciliation between the opening equity balances and the closing equity balances.

▸ **Detailed notes on accounting policies**
These must include information that is required by other IFRS but not contained in the financial statements. There must be a note to describe the cases where management has used their judgment in applying accounting policies that have a significant impact on items in the financial statements.

Also, when financial statements are reclassified or restated or there is a change in accounting policy, an additional statement of financial position must be included in the financial statements for the start of the earliest comparative period.

In addition, there must be a statement that the financial statements comply with IFRS, but this statement can only be included if the financial statements comply with all IFRS.

IAS 1 states that all financial statements are prepared on a:

- **Going concern basis**
  The company can continue trading in the foreseeable future.
- **Accrual basis**
  Transactions are recognized as they occur, not when they are actually paid for.

Finally, the standard states that financial statements must be prepared annually.

SAP Components Impacted

Similar to IFRS 1, this standard impacts all SAP financial reporting. The main SAP components impacted include SAP General Ledger, consolidation and reporting and analytic tools.

2.2.10 IAS 2: Inventories

This standard describes the accounting treatment for inventories.

Key Points

The challenge for inventory valuation is to determine the cost that inventory should be recorded at in the statement of financial position. IAS 2 states that the inventories must be valued at the lower of cost and net realizable value (NRV).

Costs should include all costs of purchase, costs of conversion, and other costs incurred in bringing the inventory to its present location and condition.

NRV is the estimated selling price of the inventory in the ordinary course of business less the estimated costs of making the sale.

One important point to note in this standard is that for inventories that cannot be individually identified, costs must be determined on a first in, first out (FIFO) basis or a weighted average basis. IAS 2 does not permit the last in, first out (LIFO) valuation.

When inventories are sold, the costs must be recognized in the same period as the revenues.

SAP Components Impacted

The main SAP component impacted is materials management and, specifically, inventory management. Other SAP components include SAP General Ledger, asset management, consolidation and reporting and analytics.

> **Note**
>
> For U.S. companies that use the LIFO valuation, significant changes will be required in their SAP system.

2.2.11 IAS 7: Cash Flow Statements

This standard requires information on the changes in cash and cash equivalents during the period. The cash flows must be from operating, investing, and financing activities.

Key Points

The standard defines cash equivalents as short-term, highly liquid investments that can easily be converted to cash without a significant change in value.

The purpose of the cash flow statement is to provide users of the financial statements with information on a company's ability to generate cash and cash equivalents.

For operating activities, a company can use two methods to report cash flows:

▶ **Direct method**
  This is the recommended approach where major cash receipts and cash payments are presented.

▶ **Indirect method**
  With this method, the profit or loss from the income statement is adjusted for noncash items such as accruals and items relating to financing activities.

Cash flows from investing activities must be presented separately and include the acquisition and disposal of long-term assets. Cash flows from the acquisition or disposal of business subsidiaries must be presented under investing activities with additional disclosure.

Cash flows from financing activities must also be presented separately. These include any activities that cause a change in a company's equity or debt.

Investing or financing activities that do not involve cash or cash equivalents do not require a cash flow statement but must still be disclosed.

SAP Components Impacted

The main SAP components impacted include SAP General Ledger, accounts receivable, accounts payable, consolidation and reporting and analytics.

2.2.12   IAS 8: Accounting Policies, Changes in Accounting Estimates, and Errors

This standard describes how to select accounting policies and the required accounting treatment of changes in accounting policies.

Key Points

The standard states that accounting policies must be selected by using IFRS. When there is not an applicable IFRS, management must use its judgment in creating an accounting policy but should consider the following:

▶ Other IFRS that deal with similar or related issues

▶ Definitions and guidance in the Framework for the Preparation and Presentation of Financial Statements

Accounting policies must be applied consistently. A company can only change an accounting policy under the following circumstances:

▶ It is required to by an IFRS.

▶ It will result in the financial statements providing more relevant and reliable information.

If a change in accounting policy is required owing to a new IFRS, a company need only make the change from the date that the IFRS is first applicable. However, other changes in accounting policies must be applied retrospectively from the earliest past period possible.

Changes in accounting estimates such as asset useful lives do not need to be applied retrospectively — just from the current period.

Any material errors resulting from accounting policies being applied incorrectly or fraud, for example, must be corrected and applied retrospectively from the earliest past period possible.

SAP Components Impacted

The main SAP components impacted include consolidation and reporting and analytics.

2.2.13   IAS 10: Events after the Balance Sheet Date

This standard describes when a company should adjust its financial statements for events after the balance sheet date and the associated disclosures required.

Key Points

Events after the balance sheet date are defined as events occurring between the end of the company's fiscal year and the date when the financial statements were authorized to be issued.

The standard defines two kinds of events:

▶ **Adjusting events**
Events that must be adjusted for in the financial statements. These are events that provide evidence of conditions that existed at year end.

▶ **Nonadjusting events**
Events that should not be adjusted in the financial statements. These are events due to conditions after the year-end such as changes in exchange rates.

If the events after the balance sheet date are so significant that after adjustment, the financial statements are no longer prepared on a going concern basis, a company cannot issue the financial statements on a going concern basis.

SAP Components Impacted

The main SAP components impacted include consolidation and reporting and analytics.

2.2.14 IAS 11: Construction Contracts

This standard describes the accounting treatment for construction contracts in the financial statements of the construction contractor.

Key Points

The standard explains how to account for the revenue and expenses incurred during a construction contract. Owing to the length and nature of construction contracts, revenues and expenses are often incurred in different accounting periods.

Contract revenue includes the initial revenue agreed in the contract and any variations in contract work, claims, and incentive payments when they will likely result in revenue and can be reliably measured.

Contract costs include costs related directly to the contract, costs from general contract activity, and other costs that are chargeable to the customer under the terms of the contract.

When the outcome of the construction contract can be estimated reliably, revenues and costs must be recognized by reference to the stage of completion of the contract.

When the outcome of the construction contract cannot be estimated reliably, contract costs are recognized at the time that they are incurred, and revenue is only recognized when costs incurred are expected to be recovered.

When it is estimated that contract costs will exceed contract revenue, the expected loss must be recognized as an expense immediately.

SAP Components Impacted

The main SAP components impacted may include SAP General Ledger, project systems, internal orders, consolidation and reporting and analytics.

2.2.15 IAS 12: Income Taxes

This standard describes the accounting treatment for income taxes. Income taxes include domestic and foreign taxes and withholding taxes paid by subsidiaries of the reporting entity on distributions to the reporting entity.

Key Points

The standard explains how to account for the current and future tax consequences of:

▶ The future recovery (settlement) of assets and liabilities shown in a company's statement of financial position

▶ Transactions and other events of the current period that are shown in the financial statements

Taxes for the current or past periods must be shown as either an asset or a liability in the financial statements, measured at the amount that is expected to be recovered (asset) or settled (liability).

If it is expected that the future recovery of assets and settlement of liabilities will result in larger (or smaller) taxes, a company must include a deferred tax liability (or asset) in its financial statements.

The deferred tax asset or liability must be measured using the tax rate that is expected when the asset is recovered or the liability is settled.

The carrying amount of a deferred tax asset must be reviewed each year on the date of the statement of financial position.

Deferred assets or liabilities cannot be classified as current in the statement of financial position.

SAP Components Impacted

The main SAP components impacted include SAP General Ledger, consolidation and reporting and analytics.

2.2.16   IAS 16: Property, Plant, and Equipment

This standard describes the accounting treatment for property, plant, and equipment.

Key Points

The standard defines property, plant, and equipment as tangible items that:

▶ Are held for use in the production or supply of goods and services, for rental to others, or for administrative purposes

▶ Are expected to have a useful life greater than one year

The cost of property, plant, and equipment can only be recognized as an asset if:

▶ Future economic benefits will pass to the company

▶ The cost can be measured reliably

The cost of an asset includes all costs incurred in preparing the asset for its intended use.

The standard defines two models for the carrying value of an asset:

▶ **Cost model**
The asset is valued at its cost less accumulated depreciation and impairment.

▶ **Revaluation model**
The asset is valued at a revalued amount that is its fair market value at the date of revaluation less subsequent depreciation and impairment.

If the use of the revaluation model results in an increase over the existing value of the asset, the revaluation surplus must be credited to equity.

If the use of the revaluation model results in a decrease over the existing value of the asset, the revaluation decrease must be expensed in the income statement.

If there is a revaluation surplus on an asset that previously had a revaluation decrease that was expensed in the income statement, the surplus must first be credited to the income statement until the decrease is offset.

If there is a revaluation decrease on an asset that previously had a revaluation surplus that was credited to equity, the decrease must first be debited to equity until the surplus is offset.

Depreciation is defined as a systematic charge over an asset's useful life. The depreciation method used must reflect how the company will use the asset's future economic benefits.

The standard requires separate depreciation for each component part of property and equipment when the component part's cost is significant relative to the total cost.

SAP Components Impacted

The main SAP component impacted is asset management. Other components impacted include SAP General Ledger, project systems, internal orders, materials management, consolidation and reporting and analytics.

> **Note**
>
> For companies that must now depreciate assets at the component level as per IAS 16, there will be significant changes to asset master data.

2.2.17 IAS 17: Leases

This standard describes the accounting treatment for finance and operating leases to be used by both lessors and lessees.

Key Points

The standard states that a lease can be either a finance or operating lease:

▶ **Finance lease**
Almost all risks and rewards of ownership are passed to lessee.

▶ **Operating lease**

All other leases in cases where almost all risks and rewards of ownership are not passed to lessee.

The accounting treatment for lessees is as follows:

▶ **Finance lease**

A finance lease must be shown as an asset or liability in the statement of financial position. The value of the asset or liability must be lower than the fair value of the leased property and the present value of the future minimum lease payments.

▶ **Operating lease**

All lease payments must be expensed on a straight line basis over the lease term.

The accounting treatment for lessors is as follows:

▶ **Finance lease**

A finance lease must be shown as a receivable under assets in the statement of financial position. The value of the receivable should be equal to the net investment in the lease. Finance income relating to the lease must be based on a pattern reflecting a constant periodic rate of return on the lessors' net investment in the lease.

▶ **Operating lease**

Assets held for operating leases must be shown as assets in the statement of financial position under the applicable asset category. They must then be depreciated depending on the rules for assets in that category. Income from the lease payments must be shown on a straight line basis over the lease term.

The accounting for sale and leaseback transactions depends on whether they meet the criteria for finance or operating leases as shown above.

SAP Components Impacted

The main SAP component impacted is asset management. Other components impacted include SAP General Ledger, consolidation and reporting and analytics.

2.2.18 IAS 18: Revenue

This standard describes the accounting treatment of revenue, particularly when to recognize revenue. Revenue includes income from sale of goods, provision of services, and finance income such as interest, royalties, and dividends.

Key Points

The standard states that revenue must be valued at the fair value of the amount received or the receivable. Fair value is defined as the amount at which an asset could be exchanged or a liability settled by two knowledgeable parties in an arm's length transaction.

The main focus of this standard is when to recognize revenue. Revenue can only be recognized when it is probable that the economic benefits will flow to the seller, but there are other factors depending on the type of revenue as follows:

▸ **Sale of goods**
Revenue must be recognized when the significant risks and rewards of ownership of the goods have passed to the buyer and when the amount of revenue can be reliably measured.

▸ **Provision of services**
Revenue must be recognized in relation to the stage of completion of the service at the statement of financial position date.

▸ **Interest, royalties, and dividends**
Interest must be recognized using the effective interest method described in IAS 39. Royalties must be recognized on an accrual basis depending on the royalty agreement. Dividends must be recognized when it is the shareholders right to receive the dividend.

SAP Components Impacted

The main SAP components impacted include SAP General Ledger, accounts receivable, sales and distribution, consolidation and reporting and analytics.

2.2.19 IAS 19: Employee Benefits

This standard describes the accounting treatment of employee benefits. Employee benefits include all payments made to employees in exchange for services. This includes wages, bonuses, pensions, profit sharing, disability, and so on.

Key Points

Employee benefits must be recognized when a company receives the service from the employee and not when the benefits are paid or are payable.

Benefits that are payable after a service has been provided must be shown as an accrual liability in the statement of financial position. Benefits that have been paid after a service was provided must be expensed.

Benefits such as profit sharing and bonuses must only be recognized when a company legally has to pay them and they can be measured reliably.

Postemployment benefits such as pensions must be classified as either of the following:

▸ **Defined contribution plan**
 A company makes fixed contributions to a separate fund and has no other obligation other than the agreed amount to be contributed to the fund. Contributions must be expensed in the period in which the contribution is payable.

▸ **Defined benefit plan**
 A company has an obligation to provide an agreed benefit to employees. Using actuarial methods, a company must estimate the amount of benefit payable and show this amount as a liability in the statement of financial position. The total liability is equal to the total of the current fair value of assets in the plan plus the present value of future obligations plus the deferred actuarial gains and losses.

Actuarial gains and losses arising from long-term employee benefits other than postemployment benefits may be recognized immediately.

Termination benefits must be recognized when a company has committed to terminate an employee and to provide termination benefits.

SAP Components Impacted

The main SAP components impacted include SAP General Ledger, human resources, consolidation and reporting and analytics.

2.2.20 IAS 20: Accounting for Government Grants and Disclosure of Government Assistance

This standard describes the accounting treatment for government grants and disclosure of government assistance.

Key Points

A government grant may be in monetary form or be nonmonetary in the form of an asset. All monetary and nonmonetary grants (at fair value) cannot be recognized until it is reasonable to assume that a company will comply with the conditions for obtaining the grant and that the grant will be received.

Grants relating to income must be shown as income and recognized on a systematic basis to match the related costs that they are intended to compensate.

Grants relating to assets must be shown as deferred income or as a deduction to the value of the related asset.

When a government grant is repayable, it must be treated as a revision of an accounting estimate in accordance with IAS 8.

2.2.21 IAS 21: The Effects of Changes in Foreign Exchange Rates

This standard describes the accounting treatment for foreign currency transactions.

Key Points

The standard states that a company's functional currency is the currency of the primary economic environment in which it operates. This should be the currency in which a company determines its sales prices, material costs,and so on.

A foreign currency is any currency other than the functional currency, and all foreign currency must be translated into the functional currency.

All foreign currency transactions must be translated at the exchange rate on the date of the transaction and then at the end of each reporting period:

▶ Nonmonetary items recorded at historical costs such as assets can remain at historical cost.

▶ Nonmonetary items recorded at fair value in foreign currency must be translated at the exchange rate when the fair value was determined.

▶ Monetary items must be translated using the exchange rate on the closing day of the reporting period.

Exchange differences from the settlement or translation of monetary items must be shown in the statement of comprehensive income in the period that the settlement or translation occurs.

Exchange differences arising from the translation of investment in a foreign operation should also be shown in the statement of comprehensive income for the individual financial statements but as a component of equity in the consolidated financial statements. On disposal of the foreign operation, the exchange differences are reclassified from equity to the statement of income.

The standard also describes how a company should translate its functional currency into another presentation currency. An example of this would be a foreign operation in Europe with a parent company in the U.S. The foreign operation would have euros as its functional currency and the U.S. dollar as its presentation currency. A company should translate its functional currency to a different presentation currency at the end of each reporting period as follows:

▶ Assets and liabilities must be translated using the exchange rate on the closing day of the reporting period.

▶ Income and expenses must be translated using the exchange rates at the date of the transactions.

▶ All exchange differences must be shown as a component of equity.

If the functional currency is the currency for a country with hyperinflation, a company must follow IAS 29.

SAP Components Impacted

The main SAP components impacted include SAP General Ledger, consolidation and reporting and analytics.

2.2.22 IAS 23: Borrowing Costs

This standard describes the accounting treatment for borrowing costs. Borrowing costs are costs incurred such as interest when borrowing funds.

Key Points

Borrowing costs are usually recognized as an expense in the period in which they are incurred. However, an exception to this is borrowing costs related to an acquisition, construction, or production of a qualifying asset that can be capitalized as follows:

▶ If funds are borrowed specifically to purchase a qualifying asset, the full amount of the borrowing costs can be capitalized less any investment income earned from investing the borrowed funds.

▶ If funds are borrowed generally and then used later to purchase a qualifying asset, the amount of the borrowing costs that can be capitalized is determined by applying a capitalization rate to the amount of the purchase.

A qualifying asset is defined as an asset that takes a substantial period of time to get ready for its intended use or sale. An example of a qualifying asset is the construction of a new manufacturing plant.

SAP Components Impacted

The main SAP components impacted include SAP General Ledger, asset management, consolidation and reporting and analytics.

2.2.23 IAS 24: Related Party Disclosures

This standard describes the disclosures that are required to show the effect of transactions with related parties on a company's financial statements.

Key Points

Another company is defined as a related party if it:

▶ Controls or is controlled by the reporting company

▶ Has significant influence over the reporting company, for example, family, key management personnel, and so on

▶ Is an associate of the reporting company as defined in IAS 28

▶ Is in a joint venture with the reporting company as defined in IAS 31

▶ Is a postemployment benefit plan for the reporting company

Disclosure is required for the following:

▶ Relationships between related parties even if there have not been any transactions

▶ Related party transactions during the period

▶ Key management personnel compensation

For related party transactions, the disclosure must include:

▶ The amounts of the transactions

▶ The outstanding balances between the related parties at the reporting date with their terms and conditions

▶ Details of any provision for doubtful debts on balances with related parties and expenses incurred from bad debts with related parties

SAP Components Impacted

The main SAP components impacted include SAP General Ledger, accounts receivable, accounts payable, consolidation and reporting and analytics.

2.2.24 IAS 26: Accounting and Reporting by Retirement Benefit Plans

This standard describes the accounting treatment for retirement benefit plans including defined contribution and defined benefit plans.

Key Points

For both types of plans the financial statements must include a statement of net assets available for benefits.

For defined benefit plans, the financial statements must also include the actuarial present value of retirement benefits showing separately vested and nonvested benefits with the resulting excess or deficit. This information can also be referenced to an attached actuarial report.

All retirement benefit plan investments must be shown at fair value.

SAP Components Impacted

The main SAP components impacted include SAP General Ledger, consolidation and reporting and analytics.

2.2.25 IAS 27: Consolidated and Separate Financial Statements

This standard describes how to prepare and present consolidated financial statements for a group of companies under the control of a parent company.

Key Points

A parent company is defined as a company that has subsidiary companies.

A subsidiary company is defined as a company that is controlled by another company.

Consolidated financial statements include the parent company and its subsidiaries and must be presented as if they are a single company.

All companies in the group must use the same accounting policies. When the consolidated financial statements are being prepared, all items such as assets, liabilities, income, and expenses are totaled. Then to present the consolidated statements as if they are a single company, the following must be eliminated:

▶ The parent's investment in subsidiaries including equity

▶ All intercompany transactions and balances

Minority interests must be shown separately under equity in the consolidated financial statements, and minority interests in the profit or loss of the group must be disclosed.

SAP Components Impacted

The main SAP components impacted include SAP General Ledger, consolidation and reporting and analytics.

2.2.26 IAS 28: Investments in Associates

This standard describes the accounting treatment for investments in associates where the investor has significant influence over the associate.

Key Points

Significant influence is defined as the power to influence financial and operating decisions of the associate. It does not mean control of the decisions.

Significant influence is assumed if the investor holds directly or indirectly 20% of the investee. It is assumed that the investor does not have significant influence if it does not hold 20% unless it can be proved otherwise.

This standard applies to all associates except for when the investor is a venture capital company, a mutual fund company, or a unit trust.

The equity method is used for investments in associates. The investment is shown initially at cost and then increased or decreased to show the investor's share of profit or loss in the associate.

The investor and associate must use the same accounting policies.

IAS 39 can be used to determine if any additional impairment loss on the investment in the associate is required.

SAP Components Impacted

The main SAP components impacted include SAP General Ledger, consolidation and reporting and analytics.

2.2.27 IAS 29: Financial Reporting in Hyperinflationary Economies

This standard describes how to prepare financial statements for a company with a functional currency that is in a hyperinflationary economy.

Key Points

The standard does not give specific circumstances for when an economy is hyperinflationary but provides the following indicators:

▸ The general population prefers nonmonetary assets or a foreign currency.

▸ Credit sales and purchases are conducted at prices to allow for inflation.

▸ Inflation has exceeded 100% over a three-year period.

Financial statements must be stated in terms of a measuring unit at the end of the reporting period. Under IAS 1 the comparative figures for previous periods must then also be restated in the measuring unit.

2.2.28 IAS 31: Interests in Joint Ventures

This standard describes the accounting treatment for interests in joint ventures.

Key Points

This standard applies to all joint ventures regardless of the structure except for when the joint venture interest is held by a venture capital company, a mutual fund company, or a unit trust.

A joint venture is defined as when two or more parties contractually agree to share control of an economic activity and when strategic and operating decisions must be unanimously approved by all parties.

The standard defines three types of joint ventures:

▸ **Jointly controlled operations**
   This is a joint venture where the parties use assets and other resources, but there is no financial structure such as a corporation. In the financial statements each party must recognize the assets that it controls and liabilities that it incurs

with respect to the joint venture and the income that it derives and expenses that it incurs from its share in the venture.

▶ **Jointly controlled assets**

This is a joint venture where assets are contributed to or acquired specifically for the joint venture. Each party receives its share of the income from the assets and must share in the expenses. In the financial statements each party must show its share of the jointly controlled assets, share of liabilities incurred, income from its share of the output of the assets with its share of the expenses, and any expenses incurred as a result of its interest in the joint venture.

▶ **Jointly controlled entities**

This is a joint venture where two or more parties establish a separate entity as a joint venture. There are two accounting treatments for jointly controlled entities:

▶ **Proportionate consolidation**

Each party's share of the jointly controlled entity, for example, assets, liabilities, income, and expenses is combined with its own financial statement line items and either presented as a total or with separate line items

▶ **Equity method**

Each party records its interest in the jointly controlled entity at cost and then adjusts for its share of future profit or loss in the entity in accordance with IAS 28

Investments in jointly controlled entities that are held for sale must be accounted for in accordance with IAS 39.

SAP Components Impacted

The main SAP components impacted include SAP General Ledger, consolidation and reporting and analytics.

2.2.29 IAS 32: Financial Instruments: Presentation

This standard describes how to show financial instruments as liabilities or equity in financial statements and how to offset them against other financial assets and financial liabilities. It complements IFRS 7 and IAS 39.

Key Points

A financial instrument must be classified as a financial asset, a financial liability, or an equity instrument on initial recognition, and the classification cannot later be changed.

Nonderivative financial instruments may contain liability and equity components.

Financial assets include cash, equity in another company, a contract to receive cash/financial assets, or non-derivative and derivative contracts.

Financial liabilities include contracts to pay another company with cash/ financial assets, nonderivative contracts where the company will have to pay with a variable amount of its own equity, and derivative contracts where the company will have to pay with a fixed amount of its own equity.

Equity instruments are contracts that refer to an interest in the company's assets after deducting all liabilities.

Interest, dividends, and gains and losses on financial instruments must be recognized as income and expenses.

A financial asset and a financial liability must be offset and the net amount shown in the financial statements only under the following circumstances:

▶ The company has a legal right to net the amounts.

▶ The company intends to settle as a net amount, that is, realize the asset and settle the liability at the same time.

SAP Components Impacted

The main SAP components impacted include SAP General Ledger, treasury, consolidation and reporting and analytics.

2.2.30 IAS 33: Earnings per Share

This standard describes how to determine and present earnings per share to improve comparisons with other companies and with other accounting periods within the same company.

Key Points

The standard applies to companies that are publicly traded, companies in the process of issuing shares, and companies who voluntarily present earnings per share.

A company must show basic and diluted earnings per share in the income statement as follows:

▶ For each class of ordinary shares that has a right to share in the profit for the period

▶ With equal prominence for all periods

▶ For discontinued operations

The calculations for basic and diluted earnings per share are as follows:

▶ **Basic**
Profit or loss for the period divided by the weighted average of ordinary shares outstanding

▶ **Diluted**
Same as basic but adjusted for the assumption that potential ordinary shares have been issued such as by convertible instruments, options, warrants, and so on

SAP Components Impacted

The main SAP components impacted include SAP General Ledger, consolidation and reporting and analytics.

2.2.31 IAS 34: Interim Financial Reporting

This standard describes the minimum content for an interim financial report and the principles for measurement and recognition for an interim financial report.

Key Points

The standard defines an interim report as either a complete or a condensed set of financial statements for an interim period. An interim period is a period less than a full financial year.

There is nothing to prevent a company from issuing a full set of financial statements for an interim period, but an interim report must at a minimum contain the following:

▶ Condensed statement of financial position

▶ Condensed statement of comprehensive income shown either as a single statement or a condensed separate income statement and a condensed statement of comprehensive income

▶ Condensed statement of changes in equity

▶ Condensed statement of cash flows

▶ Detailed notes

Materiality of items to be included in interim reports must be assessed, and the standard recognizes that estimates may be required.

Interim reports must use the same accounting policies as the annual financial statements except for when policies have changed since the last annual statements.

SAP Components Impacted

The main SAP components impacted include SAP General Ledger, asset management, materials management, sales and distribution, consolidation and reporting and analytics.

2.2.32 IAS 36: Impairment of Assets

This standard describes the accounting treatment for impairment of assets that occurs when an asset's carrying value is greater than its recoverable amount.

Key Points

An impairment loss must be recognized when an asset's carrying value is greater than its recoverable amount.

Recoverable amount is defined as the higher amount that an asset would sell for less selling costs and the asset's value in use. Value is use is the present value of expected future cash flows from the asset.

At the end of each reporting period, a company must assess the values of each of its assets to see if there is impairment. If there is impairment, it must then calculate the recoverable amount.

If an asset is impaired, it must be written down to its recoverable amount, and the impairment loss must be expensed in the statement of income. An exception to this is if the asset has previously been revalued, and then the impairment loss must be treated as a revaluation decrease.

SAP Components Impacted

The main SAP components impacted include SAP General Ledger, asset management, consolidation and reporting and analytics.

2.2.33 IAS 37: Provisions, Contingent Liabilities, and Contingent Assets

This standard describes the accounting treatment for all provisions, contingent liabilities, and contingent assets except from executory contracts or if covered under another standard.

Key Points

Provisions

A provision is made for a liability for a future uncertain amount with uncertain timing. A provision should be recognized in the statement of financial position when the following three conditions are true:

- A past event has caused a company to have a legal or constructive obligation.
- It is probable that the past event will cause an outflow of resources.
- The amount can be reliably estimated. A company must estimate the amount by using the amount that it would pay to settle the obligation at the reporting date or to transfer it to a third party.

At the end of each reporting period a company must review its provisions and adjust for any changes.

Contingent Liabilities

A contingent liability is caused by either of the following conditions:

► A possible future obligation arising from past events that is not certain at the reporting date because it depends on the outcome of other future events that are not within the total control of the company

► A present obligation arising from past events, but for which it is either not possible to reliably estimate the amount or it is not probable that there will be an outflow of resources

Contingent liabilities should not be recognized in financial statements but should be disclosed unless the probability of an outflow of resources is remote.

Contingent Assets

A contingent asset is a possible future asset arising from past events that is not certain at the reporting date because it depends on the outcome of other future events that are not within the total control of the company.

Contingent assets should not be recognized in the financial statements but must be disclosed.

SAP Components Impacted

The main SAP components impacted include SAP General Ledger, materials management, sales and distribution, consolidation and reporting and analytics.

2.2.34 IAS 38: Intangible Assets

This standard describes the accounting treatment of intangible assets that are not covered under another standard.

Key Points

The standard defines an intangible asset as a nonmonetary asset without physical substance.

An intangible asset must be recognized if both of the following conditions are met:

▶ It is probable that future economic benefits from the asset will flow to the company.

▶ The cost of the asset can be reliably measured.

When intangible assets are acquired as a result of a business combination, they must be recognized at fair value and shown separately to goodwill. An example of this is research and development.

Other intangible assets should be initially recognized at cost.

Internally generated goodwill and internal research can never be recognized as intangible assets. Research costs must be expensed.

Development costs can be recognized as an intangible asset if specific criteria are met. These include whether the development will create future economic benefits, the intention to complete the development, and so on.

A company may choose to account for intangible assets under the cost model or the revaluation model:

▶ **Cost model**
  The intangible asset should be shown at cost less accumulated amortization and accumulated impairment losses.

▶ **Revaluation model**
  The intangible asset should be shown at its fair value at the date of revaluation less subsequent accumulated amortization and subsequent accumulated impairment losses.

The useful life of an intangible asset may be finite or indefinite. An intangible asset only has an indefinite useful life when there is no foreseeable limit for the periods that the asset will provide net cash inflows for the company.

Intangible assets with finite useful lives must be amortized over their useful life. Amortization should start when the asset is first available for use, and unless a more suitable pattern can be determined, the straight line method should be used.

Intangible assets with indefinite useful lives are not amortized but must be reviewed annually for impairment in accordance with IAS 36.

SAP Components Impacted

The main SAP components impacted include SAP General Ledger, asset management, consolidation and reporting and analytics.

2.2.35   IAS 39: Financial Instruments: Recognition and Measurement

This accounting standard describes how to recognize and measure financial assets and financial liabilities. The presentation of financial instruments was covered under IAS 32.

Key Points

A company must recognize all financial instruments in its statement of financial position when the company becomes a party to the contractual provisions of the instrument.

Financial assets and financial liabilities must be initially measured at fair value.

After the initial measurement at fair value, financial assets including derivatives that are assets should continue to be measured at fair value except in the following cases:

▶ **Loans and receivables**
Measured at amortized cost

▶ **Held to maturity investments**
Measured at amortized cost

▶ **Assets that cannot be reliably measured**
Measured at cost, for example, investments in equity instruments that do not have a quoted market price

All financial assets except those measured at fair value in the statement of income must be reviewed for impairment.

After the initial measurement at fair value, financial liabilities must be measured at amortized cost. Exceptions that must be measured at fair value include the following:

- ▸ Derivative liabilities
- ▸ Financial liabilities that are measured at fair value through the statement of income
- ▸ Financial guarantee contracts

Gains and losses from changes in fair value of financial instruments must be treated as follows:

- ▸ Gains and losses on financial assets or liabilities measured at fair value through the statement of comprehensive income.
- ▸ Gains and losses on financial assets that are available for sale through the statement of changes of equity. When the assets are derecognized, the cumulative gain or loss must then be recognized in the statement of comprehensive income.

The standard defines when financial assets and financial liabilities must be derecognized and removed from the statement of financial position. If a company no longer has ownership of future cash flows from the asset, the asset should be derecognized. However, if a company has not substantially transferred all risks and rewards and control of the asset, it must continue to recognize the asset.

Hedging is permitted, and the standard defines three types of hedges:

- ▸ **Fair value hedge**
  This is a hedge against a change in fair value of a recognized asset or liability or an unrecognized firm commitment. Changes in the fair values of the hedge instrument and the asset or liability must be recognized in the statement of income.

- ▸ **Cash flow hedge**
  This is a hedge against changes in future cash flows relating to a recognized asset or liability or a highly probable forecast transaction. Any gain or loss on the hedging instrument that is an effective hedge must be recognized in equity. Any gain or loss from an ineffective hedge must be recognized in the statement of income.

- ▸ **Hedges on investments in foreign operations**
  These must be treated the same way as cash flow hedges.

SAP Components Impacted

The main SAP components impacted include SAP General Ledger, treasury, consolidation and reporting and analytics.

2.2.36 IAS 40: Investment Property

This standard describes the accounting treatment for investment property and its related disclosure.

Key Points

The standard defines investment property as land or buildings that are owned (or held by a lessor under a finance lease) for the purpose of obtaining rental income and/or capital appreciation.

Investment property can only be recognized as an asset when it is probable that the future economic benefits will flow to the company and that the cost of the property can be reliably measured.

Investment property must be initially recognized at cost including transaction costs.

There are two permitted methods for accounting for the property:

► **Cost model**
The investment property is recorded at cost less depreciation less impairment losses.

► **Fair value model**
The investment property is recorded at fair value with any future changes in fair value recognized in the statement of income

Whichever model is chosen must be applied to all investment property.

Investment property must be derecognized when it is sold or when a company does not expect to receive any future economic benefits.

SAP Components Impacted

The main SAP components impacted include SAP General Ledger, asset management, consolidation and reporting and analytics.

2.2.37 IAS 41: Agriculture

This standard describes the accounting treatment for a company engaging in agricultural activity.

Key Points

The standard defines agricultural activity as the transformation of biological assets into either agricultural produce or additional biological assets.

Biological assets must be measured at fair value less estimated point of sale costs.

Agricultural produce must be measured at fair value at the point of harvest less estimated point of sale costs.

Any changes in fair values of biological assets must be immediately recognized in the statement of income.

If there is not an active market and it is therefore not possible to determine the fair value of biological assets, they may be measured at cost less accumulated depreciation less accumulated impairment losses.

This concludes the overview of the current IFRS. The next section will highlight the key differences between IFRS and local GAAPs in countries that have yet to transition to IFRS.

2.3 Differences between IFRS and Local GAAPs

Many countries that have yet to transition to IFRS have slowly been converging their local GAAP with IFRS. However, there are still many significant differences, and this section will highlight these differences for four countries that are either transitioning to IFRS at present or will be in the future. A separate book could be written on these differences, and the aim of this section is to just highlight some of the key differences that your accountants and auditors must further investigate during an IFRS project.

The four countries to be covered in this section are Chile, Brazil, Canada, and the U.S. Chile started their transition to IFRS in 2009, and we will start with it.

2.3.1 Chile

Chilean GAAP has been slowly converging with IFRS since 1997, but all major listed companies and financial institutions were required to report by IFRS from January 1, 2009. Smaller companies must report by IFRS from January 1, 2010, and private companies must continue reporting under Chilean GAAP.

Table 2.2 shows examples of differences between Chilean GAAP and IFRS.

Difference	Chilean GAAP	IFRS
Assets	Initially recognized at cost; depreciated over useful life	Initially recognized at fair value and must be depreciated by asset component parts
Goodwill from business combinations	Amortized over estimated life	Must not be amortized. Previous amortized goodwill must be reversed
Minimum dividend payable of 30%	Not shown in financial statements	Must be shown in liabilities
Deferred tax	Assets and liabilities are netted through deferred tax	No netting
Joint ventures	Shown as investments in related companies	Must be proportionately consolidated
Minority shareholding	Shown as a liability, not an equity	Must be shown as shareholders' equity

Table 2.2 Examples of Differences between Chilean GAAP and IFRS

At the time of writing, many listed companies in Chile have started reporting by IFRS.

Note

The case study in Chapter 6 is for a Chilean company called CMPC, which transitioned to IFRS on January 1, 2009, with the assistance of CAPE Global Consulting.

2.3.2 Brazil

Brazilian GAAP has also been slowly converging with IFRS, but the Brazilian SEC has defined that listed companies and financial institutions must report consolidated IFRS financial statements from January 1, 2010. Individual financial statements must still be reported by Brazilian GAAP.

In general, Brazilian GAAP requires a lower level of detail than IFRS, so there are many differences relating to disclosure. Table 2.3 shows examples of other differences between Brazilian GAAP and IFRS.

Difference	Brazilian GAAP	IFRS
Assets	Initially recognized at historical cost, but property, plant and equipment may be revalued	All assets may be revalued to fair value
Goodwill from business combinations	Amortized over estimated life not to exceed 10 years	Must not be amortized. Previous amortized goodwill must be reversed
Reporting currency	Financial statements must be prepared in local currency	Financial statements must be prepared in functional currency
Cash flow statement	Not required	Required
Consolidated financial statements	Some subsidiaries may not be consolidated	All subsidiaries must be consolidated
Consolidating foreign entities	Differences resulting from translation of balances are shown in the statement of income	Differences resulting from translation of balances are shown in equity
Deferred tax	Revaluation of land is not considered for deferred tax	Revaluation of land is considered for deferred tax
Lease	Most leases are treated as operating leases	Leases meeting the criteria for finance leases must be shown as assets
Segment reporting	Not required	IFRS 8 requires financial results for operating segments

Table 2.3 Examples of Differences between Brazilian GAAP and IFRS

> **Note**
>
> CAPE Global Consulting is presently assisting several companies in Chile and Brazil with their transition to IFRS. We have accountants on staff from Europe that have previous IFRS experience, and many of our current clients have also utilized our expertise in migrating to SAP General Ledger. By the end of 2009, we will also have offices in Canada and so will be able to offer our consulting experience to companies in both Canada and the U.S. as they start their transition to IFRS.

2.3.3 Canada

Listed companies in Canada have to report by IFRS for the period beginning January 1, 2011. On this date they must stop using Canadian GAAP, and as per IFRS 1 they must also produce comparative IFRS financial statements for 2010.

Figure 2.1 shows a roadmap for the transition to IFRS for Canadian listed companies.

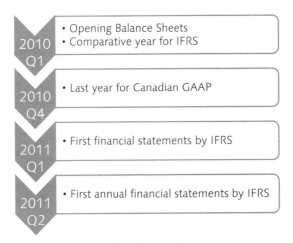

Figure 2.1 IFRS Roadmap for Canada

In May 2009, the Accounting Standards Board of Canada (AcSB) issued a bulletin stating that although current economic conditions are tough, the January 1, 2011 date is still the date for transition to IFRS. They will continue to monitor market conditions but state that Canadian GAAP now has fewer differences from IFRS than from U.S. GAAP, so Canada should proceed with the transition.

Although Canadian GAAP has been converging with IFRS, there are still some significant differences remaining. Many of the differences arise from the fact that IFRS is more principles based, whereas Canadian GAAP is more rules based. This means that IFRS is often more subjective than Canadian GAAP, and this results in increased disclosure requirements. Table 2.4 shows some examples of areas where there are differences; for a company transitioning to IFRS, these will need to be researched in detail.

Difference	CA GAAP	IFRS
Assets	For property, plant, and equipment, component accounting is rarely used	Component accounting as per IAS 16 must be used where component parts are significant
Assets (continued)	Assets cannot be revalued unless there is impairment	Assets can be revalued to fair value
Business combinations	Different rules for acquisition than IFRS 3	Acquisition method is used as per IFRS 3 with specific criteria to define a business combination
Investment property	Measured using cost	Can be measured using the cost method or fair value method
Leases	Different rules for defining finance leases	Leases must be classified as finance leases when a company has risks and rewards of ownership

Table 2.4   Examples of Differences between Canadian GAAP and IFRS

2.3.4   United States

Chapter 1, Section 1.5.1 discussed the current status of IFRS for the U.S. The SEC has proposed a roadmap indicating that listed U.S. companies will be required to report by IFRS in 2014, but this has not been finalized.

This section, however, will focus on the current differences between U.S. GAAP and current IFRS. Similar to CA GAAP, U.S. GAAP is more rules based than IFRS, so IFRS will require additional disclosure. Table 2.5 shows examples of significant differences that exist at the time of writing.

Difference	U.S. GAAP	IFRS
Fixed assets	Impairment losses are permanent Does not allow revaluation to fair value Does not require component accounting for depreciation	If specific criteria are met, impairment losses can be reversed Impairment may occur earlier than U.S. GAAP Permits revaluation to fair value Requires component accounting for depreciation
Intangible assets	Development costs must generally not be capitalized	If specific criteria are met, development costs must be capitalized
Inventory	Permits last in, first out costing	Last in, first out costing is not permitted
Financial assets	Easier to derecognize financial assets	Can only derecognize if almost all of the risks and rewards have been transferred
Leases	Specific criteria for determining types of leases	More subjective; depends on when risks and rewards of ownership are passed to the lessor
Revenue recognition	More rules for revenue recognition than IFRS. Incremental cost model allowed for customer loyalty programs. Revenue from service contracts cannot be recognized on a percentage of completion basis	Incremental cost model is not allowed under IFRS. Revenue from service contracts must be recognized on a percentage of completion basis

Table 2.5 Examples of Differences between U.S. GAAP and IFRS

There are many other differences in addition to the examples shown in Table 2.5 such as in the areas of tax, provisions, expense recognition, and so on, but it is beyond the scope of this book to cover all of the differences in detail. Many other books are available that discuss these differences, and they are constantly being updated as U.S. GAAP converges with IFRS. For example, as of the time of writing there are significant differences between U.S. GAAP and IFRS for business combinations, but the issue of new guidelines for U.S. GAAP will soon eliminate them.

2.4   Summary

This chapter has provided an overview of the current accounting standards for IFRS and some examples of differences between IFRS and the local GAAPs of four countries that have yet to fully transition to IFRS. The intent of this chapter was to give SAP consultants an overview of the changes that are likely to be required in financial statements because consultants must use SAP functionality to provide solutions for these.

A good example of this is IFRS 8, Operating Segments, which this chapter covered. In the Classic general ledger it is extremely difficult to meet the requirement of IFRS 8, which is to provide financial results by segment. However, in the new SAP General Ledger, segment reporting with document splitting is a perfect solution for IFRS 8.

At the start of an IFRS project, it is the task of your internal accountants and auditors to assess your financial statements and evaluate the differences between your local GAAP and IFRS. These differences must be documented, and there should also be an assessment of their potential financial impact on the financial statements. The accounting standards are very detailed, and the accounting team must have thorough knowledge of these details to complete this task. Chapter 5 will explain the various stages in a typical IFRS project.

However, providing SAP solutions for the transition to IFRS is the main emphasis of this book, and the next two chapters will focus on this. Chapter 4 is more technical and explains upgrading to SAP ERP and migrating to SAP General Ledger. Chapter 3 describes how to configure and use the SAP functionality that is usually implemented when you transition to IFRS.

This chapter explains the SAP functionality that is available to help produce financial statements by IFRS. SAP General Ledger has the recommended functionality for IFRS including parallel ledgers, segment reporting, and document splitting, and these are the main focus of this chapter.

3 SAP ERP Financials Functionality for IFRS

3.1 Introduction

The use of SAP General Ledger means that you must have recently had a new installation of an SAP system or you have already upgraded to SAP ERP and then migrated to SAP General Ledger from the Classic general ledger. Upgrading and migration are significant projects that we will cover in Chapter 4. It is not recommended that you upgrade and migrate at the same time, and these projects can last at least six months each. In addition, a migration to SAP General Ledger can only take place at a fiscal year end, which also extends the time that it takes to have SAP General Ledger in place.

Many companies at present have a requirement to transition to IFRS and want to upgrade and migrate in the future but must find alternative means to report by IFRS in the meantime. Therefore, we will also describe in this chapter how to use the Classic general ledger to produce financial statements by IFRS.

The first topic to cover is the options for parallel reporting in SAP systems.

3.2 Parallel Reporting in SAP Systems

Parallel reporting is the ability to report financial statements by different accounting rules such as IFRS, U.S. GAAP, other local GAAPs, and so on. With the globalization of many organizations, there has always been an increased requirement to produce parallel sets of financial statements, and with the transition to IFRS most companies will require parallel reporting.

This section will explain the options that are available in the Classic general ledger and now in SAP General Ledger. The most important new functionality in SAP General Ledger is parallel ledgers, which is the recommended option for larger companies.

First, we will cover the options for parallel reporting in the Classic general ledger.

3.2.1 Parallel Reporting in the Classic General Ledger

The SAP Classic general ledger offers three options for parallel reporting, as follows:

▶ **Parallel accounts**
General ledger accounts are created and used only for postings related to the particular accounting principle. Some general ledger accounts are shared where the accounting principles are the same and the different accounting principles can be reported by grouping the general ledger accounts. Figure 3.1 shows how the general ledger common accounts are shared by U.S. GAAP, local GAAP, and IFRS reporting and how each accounting principle also has its own separate general ledger accounts. A common example is for assets that may have different useful lives depending on the accounting principle. Separate general ledger accounts are maintained for the different depreciation postings.

▶ **Special ledger**
A special ledger is maintained for reporting a different accounting principle such as IFRS. Many companies use this approach, and it is very useful for countries that have different accounting principles and require their own predefined chart of accounts.

▶ **Additional company codes**
Additional company codes are created and used just for reporting a different accounting principle such as IFRS. This option is much less used in practice than parallel accounts and the special ledger.

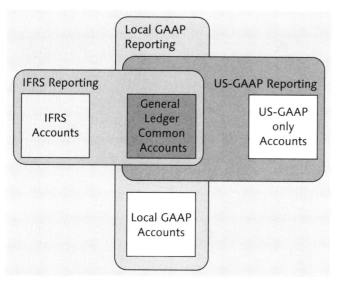

Figure 3.1 Parallel Accounts Solution

A U.S. company has a global chart of accounts but has subsidiaries in Europe — for example, France — that require local accounts to be reported to the French government using their own chart of accounts. Using a special ledger, postings made to the Classic general ledger also update a special ledger with the required local general ledger account number. Any postings unique to the French local GAAP are made directly to the special ledger.

3.2.2 Parallel Reporting in SAP General Ledger

SAP General Ledger provides two options for parallel reporting: parallel accounts as described in section 3.2.1 and parallel ledgers.

Parallel Ledgers

Parallel ledgers are a major improvement over the special ledger solution that many companies used in the Classic general ledger. Separate ledgers can be set up for each reporting requirement such as local GAAP, IFRS and, as shown in Figures

3.2 and 3.3, postings to other components, such as accounts receivable accounting, accounts payable accounting, sales and distribution, materials management, and production planning, update the ledgers simultaneously (in parallel) according to different accounting standards.

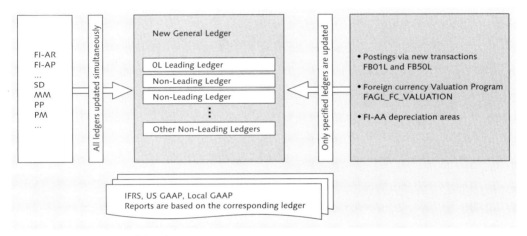

Figure 3.2 Parallel Ledgers

A *leading ledger* must be defined, which is always OL in SAP General Ledger and represents the accounting standard that the organization uses most. Other ledgers are known as *parallel (or nonleading) ledgers* and represent other accounting standards. Controlling functionality is always integrated with the leading ledger, but dimensions such as profit center accounting can be deactivated if they are not required for parallel ledgers. At present and until the U.S. starts the transition to IFRS the leading ledger OL for a U.S. company will be for U.S. GAAP, and for a European company, the leading ledger OL will usually be for IFRS.

SAP General Ledger allows the creation of multiple parallel ledgers, but, depending on an organization's requirement, usually one parallel ledger is sufficient to cover parallel reporting requirements for other countries. Having more than one parallel ledger significantly increases data volume.

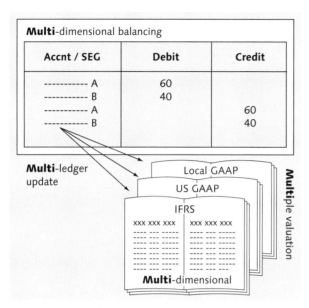

Multi-dimensional balancing		
Accnt / SEG	**Debit**	**Credit**
----------- A	60	
----------- B	40	
----------- A		60
----------- B		40

Figure 3.3 Parallel Ledgers Are Updated Simultaneously

Under the current SEC roadmap, there is a dual reporting period for U.S. companies for the years 2012 and 2013. During this time, it is possible that two parallel ledgers may be required because, for example, a subsidiary of a U.S. company may have to report by IFRS, U.S. GAAP, and its local GAAP. We discuss the options for U.S. companies in Section 3.3.

When the leading ledger is posted to, all parallel ledgers are posted to simultaneously. However, with the new posting Transactions FB01L and FB50L, postings can be made to specific parallel ledgers only (see Figure 3.4).

For example, a French subsidiary of a U.S. parent company may need to make a manual posting specific to French local GAAP requirements. In SAP ERP, this can be made in the general ledger to the specific parallel ledger L2, as shown in Figure 3.4. In the Classic general ledger using the special ledger option, the entry would have been made directly to the SPL using a different user interface, which is often confusing to users who are used to posting general ledger entries with general ledger transaction codes.

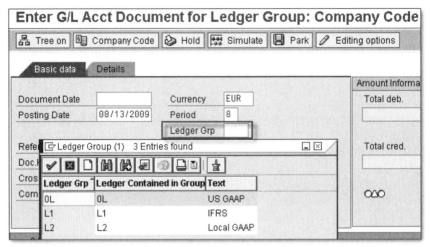

Figure 3.4 Transaction FB50L Postings to Specific Parallel Ledgers

Another example is a U.S. company that has U.S. GAAP in the leading ledger but has created a new parallel ledger for IFRS during the dual reporting period. All postings made to the U.S. GAAP leading ledger will post to the IFRS parallel ledger, but the company can then make IFRS-specific adjustments using Transactions FB01L and FB50L. At the end of the dual reporting period, adjustments must be posted to make the leading ledger for IFRS and the parallel ledger for U.S. GAAP.

Closing activities have to be run separately by parallel ledger, and SAP ERP standard reports can be run by ledger.

> **Note**
>
> The special ledger and company code options for parallel reporting are not recommended when using SAP General Ledger, so we will not consider them for the transition to IFRS in Section 3.2.3.

3.2.3 Pros and Cons of Parallel Reporting Solutions

SAP states that both the parallel accounts solution and the parallel ledgers solution are recommended for parallel reporting in SAP General Ledger. Many factors will influence this decision, and CAPE Global Consulting has found that in general, smaller companies use parallel accounts and larger companies benefit from using parallel ledgers.

In some cases the decision is easy. For example, if there is a requirement to have parallel reporting with different fiscal years, the parallel ledger approach is clearly superior. Tables 3.1 and 3.2 highlight the pros and cons for both solutions.

Parallel Accounts	
Pros	**Cons**
Ease of use and relatively simple setup	High increase in the number of general ledger accounts adding complexity to the chart of accounts
Retained earnings account and balance carry forward — separate retained earnings account for each accounting principle is maintained	Difficult to report on different fiscal years
Parallel postings in the specific account areas	Postings may cross valuations — for example, users may mistakenly post local GAAP to U.S. GAAP general ledger accounts. (Note: A validation is often created to ensure that cross-valuation postings do not occur)

Table 3.1 Pros and Cons of Parallel Accounts

Parallel Ledgers	
Pros	**Cons**
Fewer general ledger accounts	Data volume may increase significantly as parallel ledgers are updated simultaneously with all postings to the leading ledger
Separation of ledgers gives separate transparency (e.g., for auditors)	
Can maintain a separate ledger for each accounting principle	
Different fiscal year variants can be used for ledgers	
Different posting control variants can be used for ledgers	

Table 3.2 Pros and Cons of Parallel Ledgers

3.2.4   Setting up Parallel Accounts for IFRS

Setting up parallel accounts requires minimal configuration in SAP systems. New accounts are created in the chart of accounts that relate specifically to an accounting principle such as IFRS.

For example, a U.S. company may have its chart of accounts defined and be reporting by U.S. GAAP. If it now wants to report by IFRS using parallel accounts. it must follow these steps:

1. **Identify the general ledger accounts that will have differences between U.S. GAAP and IFRS.**
   An example of accounts that will generally have different balances under U.S. GAAP and IFRS rules is fixed asset accounts.

2. **Create new general ledger accounts that are specific to IFRS, usually using a different number range.**
   For example, all IFRS-specific accounts may be created in a separate number range starting with 9.

3. **Create financial statement versions to be used for U.S. GAAP and IFRS.**
   For example, financial statements by IFRS will be a mix of the common general ledger accounts and the IFRS-specific general ledger accounts.

4. **Change account determination.**
   The only configuration required for parallel accounts is changing account determination. For example, there will be separate valuation areas in asset management for U.S. GAAP and IFRS, and the valuation area for IFRS, for example, must now point to the newly created IFRS accounts.

> **Note**
>
> Many companies at present plan to upgrade to SAP ERP and then migrate to SAP General Ledger to use the parallel ledger functionality for IFRS but will not have time to do this before their IFRS deadline. CAPE Global Consulting has discussed this situation with several Canadian companies, for example, that have an IFRS deadline of January 1, 2011, but must report IFRS comparative financial statements for 2010. At the time of writing it is too late for Canadian companies to perform a technical upgrade and migration before 2010, so the best solution for producing the comparative financial statements in 2010 is to use parallel accounts.
>
> The recommended approach would thus be to perform a technical upgrade in early 2010, followed by a migration to SAP General Ledger at the end of the fiscal year using a migration scenario to switch from parallel accounts to parallel ledgers (migration scenario 4 or 5, which we will explain in Chapter 4).

Although parallel accounts are easy to set up and to understand, the parallel ledger functionality in SAP General Ledger is excellent, and it is extremely important to select the correct solution. If, for example, a company uses parallel accounts and finds that the number of general ledger accounts is too difficult to manage, a separate migration project (migration scenario 8) will be required to switch to a parallel ledger. We will cover this and other migration scenarios relevant to IFRS in Chapter 4.

3.2.5 Setting Up Parallel Ledgers for IFRS

More configuration is required to set up parallel ledgers compared to parallel accounts. Figure 3.5 shows the IMG tasks.

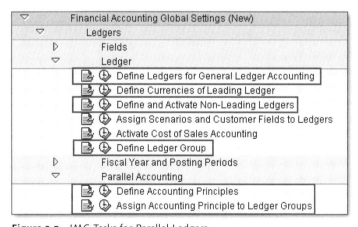

Figure 3.5 IMG Tasks for Parallel Ledgers

These four tasks are explained in the following section.

Define Ledgers for General Ledger Accounting

In general, a separate parallel ledger is required for each reporting requirement that you have in your organization. For example, a global U.S. organization that has been using an SAP system for some time has to report U.S. GAAP and local GAAPs and will now also have to report IFRS.

> **Note**
>
> For most companies that have already implemented an SAP system, the leading ledger 0L will set to their local GAAP. However, for new installations, it may make sense to set the leading ledger to IFRS. We will discuss this in Section 3.3, IFRS and Parallel Reporting Options below.

In the example of this IMG task shown in Figure 3.6, it is assumed that the leading ledger 0L is for U.S. GAAP and that there are two other parallel ledgers for IFRS and local GAAP.

In this step you need only define the parallel ledgers; 0L is specified by default as the leading ledger, and any new ledgers such as L1 and L2 are parallel ledgers (see Figure 3.6) and are named by accounting principle.

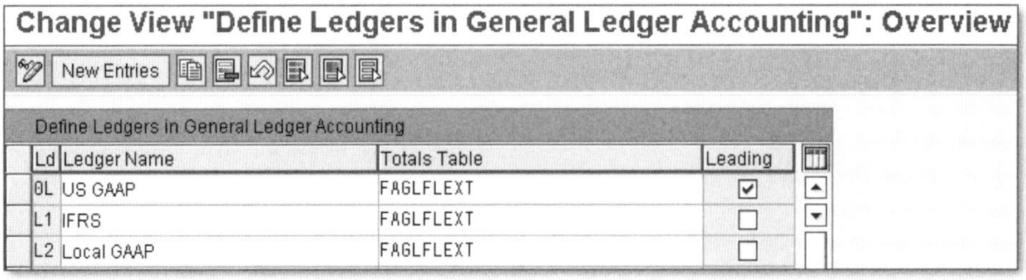

Ld	Ledger Name	Totals Table	Leading
0L	US GAAP	FAGLFLEXT	☑
L1	IFRS	FAGLFLEXT	☐
L2	Local GAAP	FAGLFLEXT	☐

Figure 3.6 Define Parallel Ledgers

Define and Activate Non-Leading Ledgers

In this step you assign company codes to the parallel ledgers. All company codes are automatically assigned to the leading ledger, and in the screen shown in Figure 3.7 you must assign all company codes to parallel ledger L1, which is for IFRS. For U.S. companies during the dual reporting period, all company codes would need to be assigned to the IFRS parallel ledger. You can also define additional currencies for the parallel ledgers, as in Figure 3.7, which shows the currency fields available.

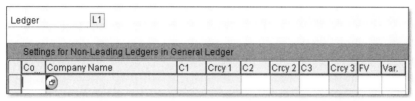

Figure 3.7 Settings for Parallel Ledgers

You may not require all currencies that are linked to the leading ledger in the parallel ledger. For example, the leading ledger may have group currency (type 30), but a parallel ledger for a local GAAP may only require local currency.

> **Note**
>
> For reporting by IFRS during the dual reporting period such as under the proposed SEC roadmap for the U.S., it is likely that you will need group currency for both IFRS and U.S. GAAP. However, other parallel ledgers for local GAAP in other countries will likely not require group currency, for example.

As shown in Figure 3.7, it is also possible to assign different fiscal year variants and posting period variants to parallel ledgers. If these fields are left blank, they default to the settings for the leading ledger.

Define Ledger Group

In this IMG task you can define ledger groups. Ledger groups allow you to combine ledgers for the purpose of joint processing. For example, you may have transactions that are only relevant for U.S. GAAP and IFRS. If you post to the leading ledger (U.S. GAAP in this example) without a ledger group, all ledgers will automatically be posted to, including the local GAAP ledger. However, it is possible to create a ledger group for U.S. GAAP and IFRS only, as shown in Figure 3.8 with ledger group L10L.

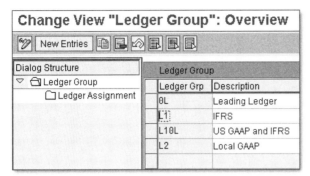

Figure 3.8 Define Ledger Groups

You must then assign the relevant ledgers to the ledger group and designate one of the ledgers as the representative ledger of the ledger group. If the leading ledger is part of the ledger group, it must always be the representative ledger. Figure 3.9 shows ledgers 0L and L1 being assigned to ledger group L10L.

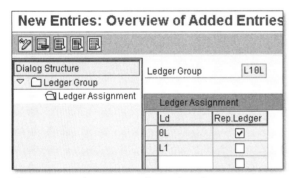

Figure 3.9 Ledgers Assigned to Ledger Group

When ledger group L10L is used in a posting now, only ledgers 0L for U.S. GAAP and L1 for IFRS will be posted to; L2 for local GAAP will be excluded.

> **Note**
>
> When you create a parallel ledger as in step 1, define ledgers for General Ledger Accounting, the system will automatically create a corresponding ledger group for the ledger. For example, the system created ledger group L1.

Define Accounting Principles

In this IMG task you must define the accounting principles that you want to use. Figure 3.10 shows an example of three accounting principles that correspond to the three ledgers as in Figure 3.6.

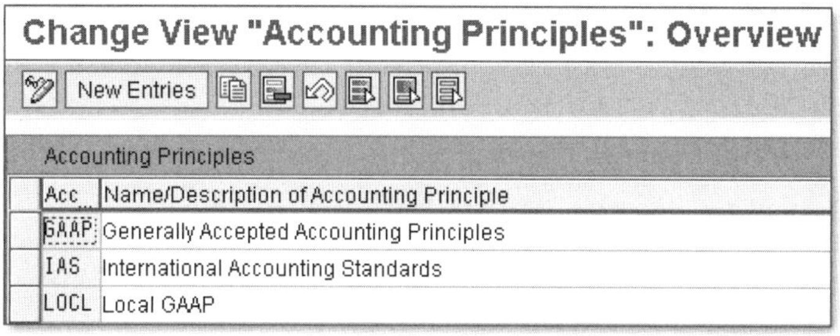

Figure 3.10 Define Accounting Principles

Assign Accounting Principle to Ledger Group

In this IMG task you must assign the accounting principles shown in Figure 3.10 to their corresponding ledgers. Figure 3.11 shows this assignment for the three accounting principles.

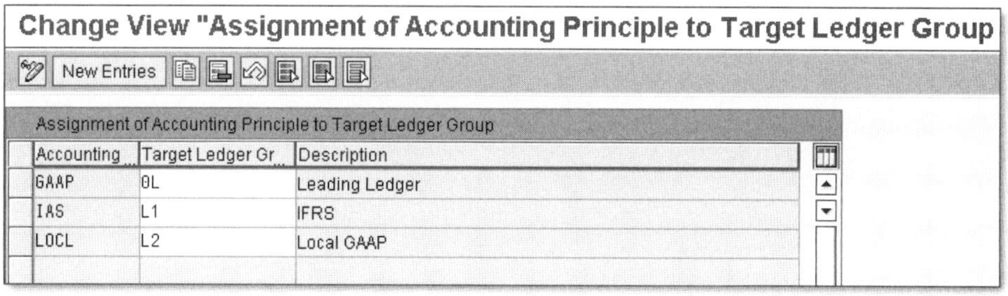

Figure 3.11 Assign Accounting Principle to Ledger Group

This section has explained parallel reporting in SAP General Ledger and how to set up parallel accounts and parallel ledgers for IFRS. The next section will explain how these parallel reporting solutions should be used for the transition to IFRS. There are different recommendations for new and existing SAP customers depending on their location and corresponding timeline for IFRS.

3.3   IFRS and Parallel Reporting Options

Many customers in various countries are asking how they should set up parallel reporting in preparation for their transition to IFRS. The answer depends on factors such as the following:

▶ Are you currently using an SAP system?

▶ What version of SAP system? Is it SAP ERP 6.0?

▶ Are you using SAP General Ledger?

▶ Does the country have a dual reporting requirement, such as the U.S.?

▶ Which solution will you use for parallel reporting? Parallel accounts or parallel ledgers?

Recommendations will be provided based on various scenarios for Latin American countries and Canada, which will be transitioning to IFRS in the near future. Separate recommendations will be provided for the U.S., which will have a dual reporting requirement in 2012 and 2013.

Sections 3.3.1 and 3.3.2 will describe scenarios for parallel ledgers, and Sections 3.3.3 and 3.3.4 will describe scenarios for parallel accounts.

3.3.1   Parallel Ledgers Scenario 1: New Implementations of SAP

In all cases, new implementations of SAP systems should implement the latest release, which is SAP ERP 6.0.

Latin America and Canada

The settings for the ledgers should be as follows:

▶ The leading ledger should be set up for IFRS.

▶ Parallel ledgers should be set up for local GAAP, tax, and so on.

▶ Asset management valuation area 01 should be set for IFRS.

> **Note**
>
> Some of our customers in Latin America have required two parallel ledgers: one for local GAAP and another for tax reporting

This is the ideal situation because there is no upgrade required and no migration required, and because all three countries will transition to IFRS in the near future, it is clear that the leading ledger must be for IFRS.

The only problem that might arise for Canada, which does not transition to IFRS until 2011, is that the IFRS accounting differences must have been determined before implementation. However, because Canadian companies are required to report comparative financial statements by IFRS in 2010, this process should have already started.

United States

This is a slightly more complex situation because the dual reporting period does not start until 2012, with IFRS officially starting in 2014.

There are two options as follows, and we will highlight the pros and cons of both.

Option 1: Leading Ledger as IFRS

The settings for the ledgers should be as follows:

▶ The leading ledger should be set up for IFRS.

▶ A parallel ledger should be set up for U.S. GAAP.

▶ Asset management valuation area 01 should be set for IFRS.

The pros and cons for U.S. companies setting the leading ledger to IFRS are shown in Table 3.3. The main con is related to the fact that the dual reporting period does not start until 2012, which is two years away, so many U.S. companies have not started identifying the differences between IFRS and U.S. GAAP.

Pros	Cons
Ledgers are set up for the future	IFRS project must have started and customer must have identified differences between IFRS and U.S. GAAP
No changeover is required for the asset management valuation area (requires systems landscape optimization (SLO) project)	2014 deadline for IFRS has not been finalized
No migration project required	

Table 3.3 Pros and Cons for U.S. Companies Using Leading Ledger for IFRS

Option 2: Leading Ledger as U.S. GAAP

The settings for the ledgers should be as follows:

► The leading ledger should be set up for U.S. GAAP.

► No parallel ledgers should be set up.

► Asset management valuation area 01 should be set for U.S. GAAP.

Under this option, the customer implements their SAP system for U.S. GAAP only. Using migration scenario 7 (see Chapter 4), the customer can later add a parallel ledger for IFRS and make accounting adjustments ready for the dual reporting period in 2012 and 2013. Table 3.4 shows the pros and cons of this option.

Pros	Cons
Longer to work on IFRS changes and more flexible if SEC changes deadline	Requires separate migration project (scenario 7)
	Requires conversion at the end of the dual reporting period to change the asset management valuation area 01 to IFRS (SLO project)
	Manual journal entries must be posted to change leading ledger to IFRS and parallel ledger to U.S. GAAP at the end of the dual reporting period

Table 3.4 Pros and Cons for U.S. Companies Using Leading Ledger for U.S. GAAP

CAPE Global Consulting recommends option 1 for U.S. customers for new implementations whenever possible. It is true that IFRS has not been finalized for the U.S., but it is coming, and option 2 requires two additional technical projects: a migration and an SLO project. There are also many adjustments that will need to be posted for the differences between IFRS and U.S. GAAP.

3.3.2 Parallel Ledgers Scenario 2: Existing Implementations of SAP System

For customers using earlier releases than SAP ERP 6.0 to use parallel ledgers, they must first upgrade to SAP ERP 6.0 and then migrate to SAP General Ledger. We will cover the upgrade and migration projects in Chapter 4.

> **Note**
>
> For customers on release SAP ERP 2004, it is still recommended that they upgrade to SAP ERP 6.0 but not required

Latin America and Canada

The settings for the ledgers should be as follows:

- ▶ The leading ledger should be set for IFRS (after migration).
- ▶ A parallel ledger should be set up for local GAAP.
- ▶ Asset management valuation area 01 should be set for IFRS.

These countries should migrate to SAP General Ledger and set up the leading ledger for IFRS and parallel ledgers for local GAAP and tax if required.

Because the deadline for IFRS is so close for these countries, the leading ledger should always be set for IFRS.

> **Note**
>
> If you want to retain the history in asset management valuation 01 for local GAAP, an SLO project will be required because valuation area 01 must now represent IFRS instead of local GAAP and be linked to the leading ledger

United States

U.S. companies are in a different situation because the IFRS deadline is 2014, but companies using earlier releases of SAP systems must start planning their upgrade and migration projects now. A migration project can only take place at a fiscal year end, so as of the time of writing the earliest that a U.S. company with a fiscal calendar year could migrate to SAP General Ledger is December 31, 2010. This must also be preceded by an upgrade project, and the latest date that the migration could take place to meet the dual reporting requirement is December 31, 2011. We will explain a proposed timeline for a U.S. company in Chapter 4.

When a U.S. company is upgrading and then migrating to SAP General Ledger as part of their IFRS project, it usually makes sense to use option 1 as in Section 3.3.1 with the settings for the ledgers as follows:

▸ The leading ledger should be set up for IFRS.

▸ A parallel ledger should be set up for U.S. GAAP.

▸ Asset management valuation area 01 should be set for IFRS.

There should be sufficient time between now and December 31, 2010 or December 31, 2011 to review the accounting differences between IFRS and U.S. GAAP.

However, U.S. companies that have recently upgraded and then migrated on December 31, 2009, for example will probably have set the leading ledger to U.S. GAAP and then will have to migrate with scenario 7 or 8 as in option 2 in Section 3.3.1 to add a parallel ledger for IFRS.

The next two sections discuss the options for using the parallel accounts solution instead of parallel ledgers.

3.3.3 Parallel Accounts Scenario 1: New Implementations of SAP System

The SAP system release should be SAP ERP 6.0 for all new implementations. Although parallel accounts are a good solution for parallel reporting, they should only be used when the differences between IFRS and the local GAAP are small, and it is recommended that larger companies use parallel ledgers,

Latin America and Canada

For companies in Latin America and Canada that want to use the parallel accounts solution, the main operating general ledger accounts should be for IFRS, and the parallel accounts should be for the local GAAP.

As explained previously, parallel accounts are usually set up in a separate number range, so Table 3.5, for example, shows how a Canadian company implementing an SAP system for the first time in 2009 or 2010 may set up the chart of accounts.

Account Number	Account Group
100000 – 199999	IFRS assets
200000 – 299999	IFRS liabilities
300000 – 399999	IFRS equity
400000 – 499999	IFRS revenue
500000 – 699999	IFRS expenses
900000 – 999999	Canadian GAAP

Table 3.5 Example of a Canadian Company's Chart of Accounts Structure with Parallel Accounts for Canadian GAAP

United States

Similar to the options for parallel ledgers in Section 3.3.1, companies in the U.S. that want to use parallel accounts have two options.

Option 1: Main Accounts as IFRS with Parallel Accounts for U.S. GAAP

With this option the accounts would be set up with main accounts for IFRS and parallel accounts for U.S. GAAP. Table 3.6 shows an example account structure for a U.S. company.

Account Number	Account Group
100000 – 199999	IFRS assets
200000 – 299999	IFRS liabilities
300000 – 399999	IFRS equity
400000 – 499999	IFRS revenue
500000 – 699999	IFRS expenses
900000 – 999999	U.S. GAAP

Table 3.6 Example of a U.S. Company's Chart of Accounts Structure with Parallel Accounts for U.S. GAAP

The pros and cons for U.S. companies setting the main accounts to IFRS are shown in Table 3.7.

Pros	Cons
IFRS accounts are set up as they will be used in the future	IFRS project must have started, and customer must have identified differences between IFRS and U.S. GAAP
No changeover is required for the asset management valuation area (requires SLO project)	2014 deadline for IFRS has not been finalized

Table 3.7 Pros and Cons for U.S. Companies Using Main Accounts for IFRS

Option 2: Main Accounts as U.S. GAAP with Parallel Accounts for IFRS
With this option the accounts would be set up with parallel accounts for IFRS. Table 3.8 shows an example account structure for a U.S. company.

Account Number	Account Group
100000 – 199999	U.S. GAAP assets
200000 – 299999	U.S. GAAP liabilities
300000 – 399999	U.S. GAAP equity
400000 – 499999	U.S. GAAP revenue
500000 – 699999	U.S. GAAP expenses
900000 – 999999	IFRS

Table 3.8 Example of a U.S. Company's Chart of Accounts Structure with Parallel Accounts for IFRS

The pros and cons for U.S. companies setting the main accounts to U.S. GAAP are shown in Table 3.9.

Pros	Cons
Longer to work on IFRS changes and more flexible if SEC changes deadline	Requires conversion at the end of the dual reporting period to change the asset management valuation area 01 to IFRS (SLO project)
	Manual journal entries must be posted to change main accounts to IFRS and parallel accounts to U.S. GAAP at the end of the dual reporting period

Table 3.9 Pros and Cons for U.S. Companies Using Main Accounts for U.S. GAAP

The main difference between the two options is that if U.S. GAAP is used for the main accounts now, an SLO project will still be required at the end of the dual reporting period to change the asset management valuation area 01 from U.S. GAAP to IFRS. However, the difference between the two options is less than for parallel ledgers because option 2 does not require a migration project.

3.3.4 Parallel Accounts Scenario 2: Existing Implementations of SAP System

Customers using earlier releases than SAP ERP 6.0 may or may not be using parallel accounts already. It is still recommended, however, to upgrade to SAP ERP 6.0 and then to migrate to SAP General Ledger, and there is a migration scenario specifically for this situation. Migration scenario 4, which we will cover in Chapter 4, allows a company to migrate to SAP General Ledger with parallel accounts.

Latin America and Canada

It is possible for companies in Latin America and Canada that are currently using the Classic general ledger to set up parallel accounts for IFRS without upgrading or migrating. This is not the recommended solution, but for Canadian companies, for example, that are required to report comparative IFRS statements in 2010, this may be a satisfactory interim solution. They then have the option to upgrade to SAP ERP 6.0 in 2010, followed by a migration to SAP General Ledger using migration scenario 4 at the end of the fiscal year. However, manual postings will then be required to change the main general accounts to IFRS from CA GAAP.

United States

There are again two options for U.S. companies that are currently using the Classic general ledger and want to use parallel accounts for IFRS. They can either structure their chart of accounts with the main accounts for IFRS and parallel accounts for U.S. GAAP as shown in Table 3.6, or they can structure the main accounts for U.S. GAAP and the parallel accounts for IFRS as shown in Table 3.8. If a U.S. company decides to continue using its main accounts for U.S. GAAP, it will require an SLO project to change the asset valuation area 01 from U.S. GAAP to IFRS at the end of the dual reporting period. However, if the main accounts are to be used for IFRS now, the company must have sufficient knowledge of the differences between IFRS and U.S. GAAP, but an SLO project is not required.

> **Note**
>
> If a company chooses the parallel accounts solution to meet their parallel reporting requirements and later wants to change to the parallel ledgers solution, this will require a separate migration project. Migration scenario 8, covered in Chapter 4, allows a company to add a parallel ledger while switching from parallel accounts

> **Note**
>
> CAPE Global Consulting has consulted for customers that are existing SAP customers using SAP General Ledger but have preferred to reimplement their SAP system. In one case, the customer was using SAP General Ledger but without document splitting and parallel ledgers, which is now required for IFRS. To subsequently add this functionality would require two separate migration projects (migration scenarios 6 followed by 7 or 8), both in different fiscal years. Because this would take at least 18 months in total, the customer decided to reimplement the SAP system with the correct functionality.

This section has covered parallel reporting and how it can be used for IFRS in both the Classic general ledger and SAP General Ledger. It has also explained the parallel reporting options related to IFRS for companies that are new SAP customers and for existing SAP customers.

However, other functionality in SAP General ledger such as segment reporting, document splitting, and foreign currency valuation is ideally suited for the transition to IFRS. The next section will explain the other SAP General Ledger functionality.

3.4   Other SAP General Ledger Functionality

Most companies that transition to IFRS and are using SAP General Ledger implement a parallel reporting method as described in the previous section and in addition implement segment reporting and document splitting.

This section will explain how to link the required scenarios to your leading ledger for this new functionality and will then describe the uses of segment reporting and document splitting related to IFRS and the optimal customization. Finally, this section will explain the changes to foreign currency valuation in SAP General Ledger and how to set it up for IFRS.

3.4.1 Scenarios for Leading Ledger

Section 3.2.5 explained how to set up parallel ledgers, but to be able to use functionality such as segment reporting for IFRS, you must also link the relevant scenarios to the leading ledger. Figure 3.12 shows where the scenarios are linked in the IMG.

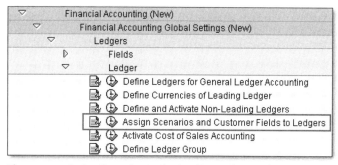

Figure 3.12 Assign Scenarios to the Leading Ledger in the IMG

SAP provides six scenarios, as shown in Table 3.10, and you cannot create new scenarios.

Scenario	Description
FIN_CCA	Cost center update
FIN_CONS	Preparations for consolidation
FIN_GSBER	Business area
FIN_PCA	Profit center update
FIN_SEGM	Segmentation
FIN_UKV	Cost of sales accounting

Table 3.10 Scenarios Available for Ledgers

The required scenarios must be assigned to the leading ledger as shown in Figure 3.13. For companies that, for example, will not be using business area functionality in SAP General Ledger, there is no need to assign scenario FIN_GSBER. Also, in general, the cost center update, scenario FIN_CCA, is usually only assigned to the leading ledger for small companies that do not use the controlling (CO) component. Data volume will be significantly increased using FIN_CCA in the leading ledger and cost center accounting in CO.

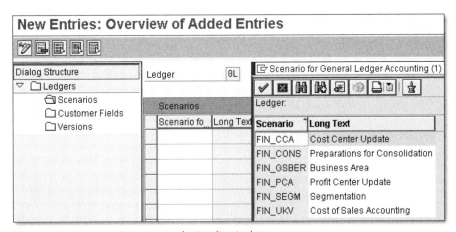

Figure 3.13 Assigning Scenarios to the Leading Ledger

Scenarios such as FIN_SEGM for segment reporting are generally not assigned to parallel ledgers because the leading ledger will be the main operational ledger and will usually be used for IFRS, whereas the parallel ledgers will be for reporting local GAAP. However, for U.S. companies that add a parallel ledger for IFRS, as in option 2 in Section 3.3.1, it may be required to add FIN_PCA and FIN_SEGM to the parallel ledger for the dual reporting period in 2012 and 2013.

3.4.2 Segment Reporting

As mentioned previously, segment reporting is now required under IFRS 8. IFRS 8 states that a company must disclose financial information for operating segments that meet specific criteria, for example, over 10% of a company's total profit or loss.

To use segment reporting in SAP General Ledger, the first step is to assign the profit center update and segmentation scenarios to the leading ledger as described in the previous section. After this, you must complete the following steps to complete the customizing for segment reporting:

▶ **Define segments**
This is an IMG task under the section shown in Figure 3.14.

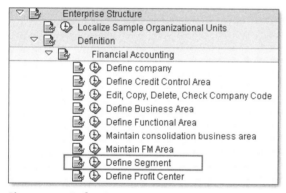

Figure 3.14 Define Segments in IMG

As per IFRS 8, segments should be set up for significant operating segments in a company. The example shown in Figure 3.15 shows segments for a forestry company that to comply with IFRS 8 will need to report financial statements for their pulp, paper, and tissue operating segments.

▶ **Derive the segments**
The most common and recommended way is to derive segments from profit centers. To do this you need to maintain the segment field on the profit centers' master records. If you are migrating to SAP General Ledger in the future, the segment field will not be available on the profit center master. To open the segment field for input, you must execute the IMG transaction shown in Figure 3.16.

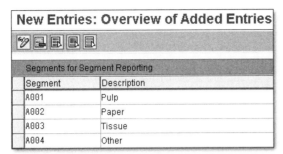

Figure 3.15 Example of New Segments for Forestry Company

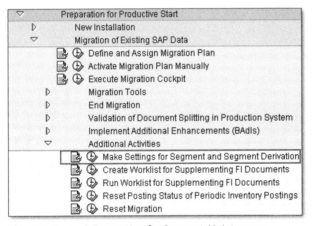

Figure 3.16 IMG Transaction for Segment Maintenance

Figure 3.17 shows the options available for segment maintenance and derivation. Selecting the Maintain Segment checkbox allows the segment field to be maintained on the profit center master record as shown in Figure 3.18. Selecting the Seg. Derivatn Active checkbox starts deriving segments when profit centers are posted to.

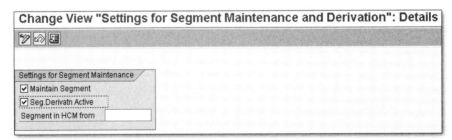

Figure 3.17 Segment Maintenance and Derivation

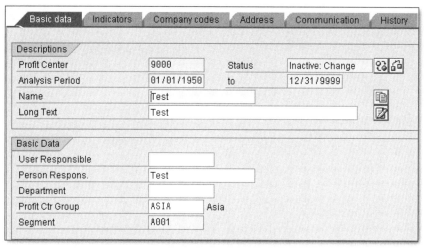

Figure 3.18 Segment Field on Profit Center Master Record

▶ **Maintain the field status group linked to general ledger account master records**

For all general ledger accounts for which you require segment postings, you should make the segment field optional in the field status groups. The segment field is in the additional account assignments section of the field status as shown in Figure 3.19.

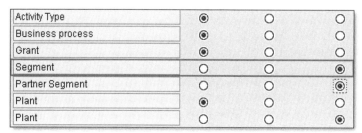

Figure 3.19 Segment Field as Optional in Field Status Group

▶ **Maintain the field status groups of posting keys for postings to the segment field**

Similar to Figure 3.19, the segment field in the field status for posting keys must also be set as optional.

This section has described how to set up segment reporting in SAP General Ledger. There is other functionality called document splitting, which is often used in conjunction with segment reporting to produce fully balanced financial statements by segment. We will explain document splitting in the following section.

3.4.3   Document Splitting

Document splitting functionality allows a company to produce fully balanced financial statements at lower levels than company code. You can select SAP fields such as segment, profit center, business area, and so on as document splitting characteristics. You can then activate a function called zero balancing to produce fully balanced financial statements by the document splitting characteristic.

Many companies that are either implementing SAP General Ledger as a new installation or migrating from the Classic general ledger use segment as the document splitting characteristic to meet the IFRS 8 requirements.

> **Note**
>
> Before SAP General Ledger was introduced, document splitting functionality was only available in the SAP Enterprise release, and it required the use of a special purpose ledger.

This section will start by explaining how to customize document splitting. Figure 3.20 shows the IMG tasks for document splitting.

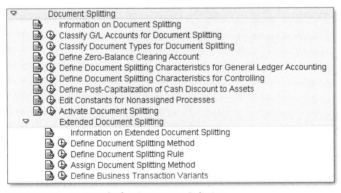

Figure 3.20   IMG Tasks for Document Splitting

Document Splitting Customization

The key IMG tasks required for customization of document splitting are as follows:

▶ **Classify G/L Accounts for Document Splitting**
The first step, and one of the most important for document splitting, is to assign general ledger accounts to an item category. Document splitting requires all accounts to have an item category, and whereas the system can automatically determine the item category for some accounts such as customer reconciliation accounts, it cannot for others such as cash accounts. Therefore, the first IMG task is Classify G/L Accounts for Document Splitting as shown in Figure 3.21.

Acct from	Account to	Overrd.	Cat.	Description	
111000	119999	☐	04000	Cash Account	
120000	330000	☐	01000	Balance Sheet Account	
410000	440030	☐	30000	Revenue	
500000	699999	☐	20000	Expense	

Figure 3.21 Classify G/L Accounts for Document Splitting

As mentioned previously, the system can determine some types of accounts, but Figure 3.21 shows the minimum that must be maintained. Cash, balance sheet, revenue, and expense accounts must be classified in this table because the system has no other way of identifying them.

▶ **Classify Document Types for Document Splitting**
All document types must be linked to a business transaction that tells the system their purpose. The SAP-delivered document types are already set up in this table and linked to the correct business transactions, so unless you have added your own custom document types or changed the purpose of an SAP-delivered document type (not recommended) you will not need to maintain this table. KR, for example, as shown in Figure 3.22 is an SAP-delivered document type, and this is linked to business Transaction 0300, which is designated as a vendor invoice.

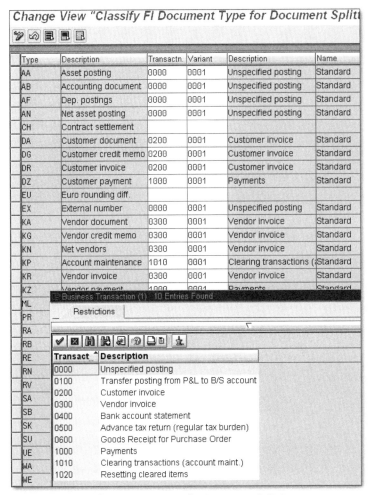

Figure 3.22 Classify Document Types for Document Splitting

▶ **Define Zero-Balance Clearing Account**

This task is only needed if you are required to produce fully balanced financial statements by your split characteristic, such as segment. If this is the case, the system ensures that each individual document posted is balanced by the split characteristic, and this requires posting of another line to a zero balance clearing account. Zero balancing is usually required for IFRS, and Figure 3.23 shows the first screen of this transaction and the fact that it is possible to change the posting keys that are used to post to the zero balance account if you have changed the standard SAP posting keys.

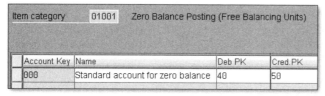

Figure 3.23 Zero Balance Account Posting Keys

Figure 3.24 shows the general ledger account that is used for zero balance posting. This general ledger account should be a clearing account.

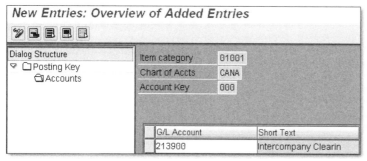

Figure 3.24 Zero Balance General Ledger Account

▶ **Define Document Splitting Characteristics for General Ledger Accounting**
This is an important step because you define the field on which you want documents to split. Figure 3.25 shows the screen, and in this example segment is the split characteristic because this will be the most common characteristic used for IFRS.

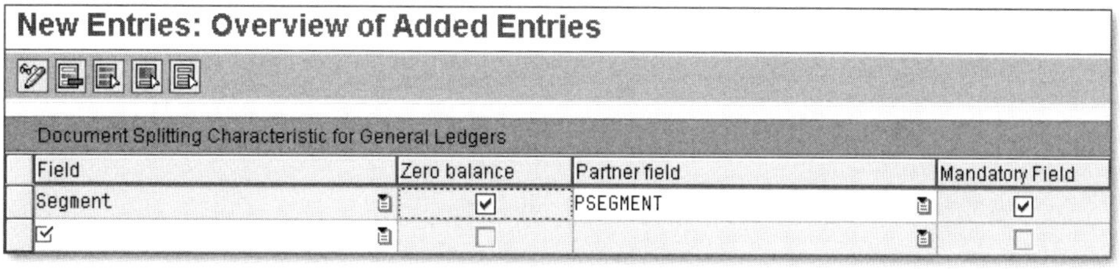

New Entries: Overview of Added Entries

Document Splitting Characteristic for General Ledgers

Field		Zero balance	Partner field		Mandatory Field
Segment		☑	PSEGMENT		☑
☑		☐			☐

Figure 3.25 Segment as Document Splitting Characteristic

It is still possible to use profit center as the document splitting characteristic and be able to produce financial statements by segments because segments are usually derived from profit centers. However, segment should be considered as the split characteristic because there are usually fewer segments than profit centers, and using segment greatly reduces your transaction data volume.

Also, the Zero Balance checkbox in Figure 3.25 has been selected, indicating that the system will balance all documents in real time by segment using the zero balance account defined in Figure 3.23. This is required to produce fully balanced financial statements by the splitting characteristic.

▶ **Define Document Splitting Method**

It is recommended that you create a custom document splitting method. In most cases, we recommend copying the standard splitting method 0000000012 and creating a new one called Z000000012

▶ **Define Document Splitting Rule**

After you create the splitting method, it must be assigned to the business transactions. Again, we recommend copying the assignments for standard splitting method 0000000012; the result is as shown in Figure 3.26

Method	Spli	Transactn.	Business transaction	Variant	Variant
Z000000012	py	0000	Unspecified posting	0001	Standard
Z000000012	Copy	0100	Transfer posting from P&L to B/S account	0001	Standard
Z000000012	Copy	0200	Customer invoice	0001	Standard
Z000000012	Copy	0300	Vendor invoice	0001	Standard
Z000000012	Copy	0400	Bank account statement	0001	Standard
Z000000012	Copy	0500	Advance tax return (regular tax burden)	0001	Standard
Z000000012	Copy	0600	Goods Receipt for Purchase Order	0001	Standard
Z000000012	Copy	1000	Payments	0001	Standard
Z000000012	Copy	1010	Clearing transactions (account maint.)	0001	Standard
Z000000012	Copy	1020	Resetting cleared items	0001	Standard

Figure 3.26 Define Document Splitting Rule

▶ **Activate Document Splitting**

The final task when the document splitting customization is complete is to activate the splitting as in Figure 3.27.

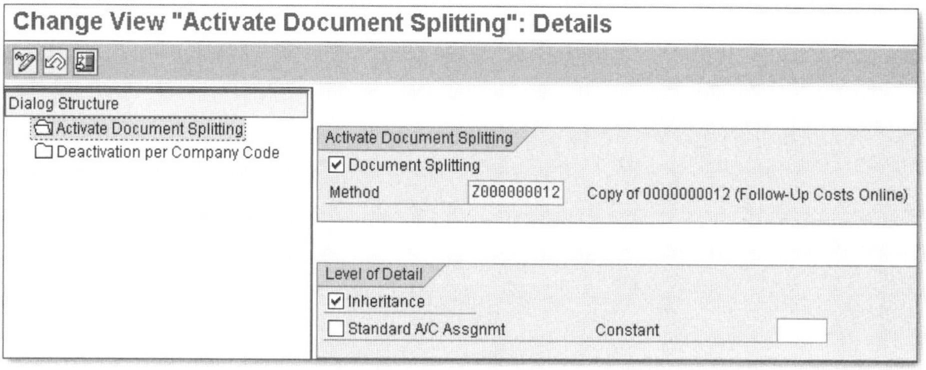

Change View "Activate Document Splitting": Details

Dialog Structure
- Activate Document Splitting
- Deactivation per Company Code

Activate Document Splitting
- ☑ Document Splitting
- Method   Z000000012   Copy of 0000000012 (Follow-Up Costs Online)

Level of Detail
- ☑ Inheritance
- ☐ Standard A/C Assgnmt   Constant

Figure 3.27 Activate Document Splitting

Figure 3.28 shows that document splitting can be deactivated for certain company codes and, as an example, company code 3000 is selected because it does not require document splitting.

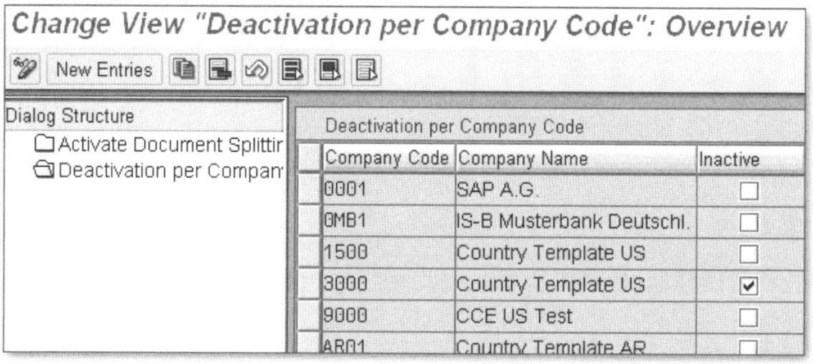

Change View "Deactivation per Company Code": Overview

New Entries

Dialog Structure
- Activate Document Splittir
- Deactivation per Compan'

Deactivation per Company Code

Company Code	Company Name	Inactive
0001	SAP A.G.	☐
0MB1	IS-B Musterbank Deutschl.	☐
1500	Country Template US	☐
3000	Country Template US	☑
9000	CCE US Test	☐
AR01	Country Template AR	☐

Figure 3.28 Deactivation of Document Splitting by Company Code

There are other document splitting customizing tasks in the IMG, but many are seldom used unless you require documents to split in different ways from the SAP standard. For example, the IMG task Define Business Transaction Variants under Extended Document Splitting shows the link between the business transactions and the general ledger item categories. Figure 3.29 shows an example of the vendor invoice business transaction 0300, and you should note that the vendor item category is required (highlighted), which means that any document posted with a KR document type requires a vendor within the document. Also, note that item category 04000 for cash accounts is not included for this business transaction, which means that you cannot post a document with a KR document type containing both a vendor and a cash account. This is standard accounting because a vendor invoice would not post to cash, and the document splitting rules help ensure that postings are correct within the system.

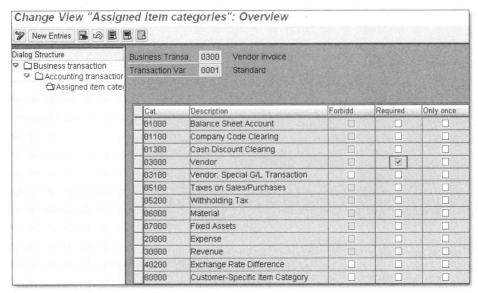

Figure 3.29 Link Between Business Transactions and Item Categories

This section has covered the customizing of document splitting, which for a migration to SAP General Ledger must be completed before the migration date (end of fiscal year). The next section will explain the effects that document splitting has on general ledger transactions.

Impact of Document Splitting on General Ledger Transactions

When SAP General ledger is active, there is an entry view of a document (linked to table BSEG for line item display) and a general ledger view (linked to table FAGLFLEXA for line item display). Figures 3.30 and 3.31 show the option to select either the entry view or the general ledger view.

When displaying a document, you also have an option to display the general ledger view as shown in Figure 3.32.

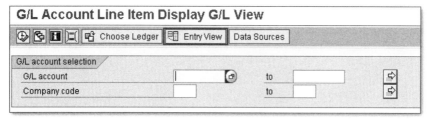

Figure 3.30 Option to Select Entry View for General Ledger Account Line Item Display

G/L Account Line Item Display Entry View

Figure 3.31 Option to Select General Ledger View for General Ledger Account Line Item Display

Figure 3.32 Display Document with General Ledger View

The entry view of a document displays a document exactly how it was entered; and Figure 3.33 shows an example. In this example, there is a customer posting with two offset postings to revenue and two different segments.

```
Doc.Type : DR ( Customer invoice ) Normal document
Doc. Number              Company code    9000       Fiscal year   2007
Doc. date     05/18/2007  Posting date   05/18/2007  Period        05
Calculate Tax
Ref.doc.      TEST SPLITTING
Doc.currency  USD
```

Itm	PK	Account	Account short text	Profit Ctr	Segment
1	01	1	Test Customer		
2	50	310000000	Revenue	P190004	NA
3	50	310000000	Revenue	P190005	EU

Figure 3.33 Entry View of a Document

Figure 3.34 shows the same document but with the general ledger view. In this example an expert view has also been selected that shows how the document splitting was derived from the configuration that was explained earlier in this chapter.

As can be seen from Figure 3.34, the customer line has now been split by segment, which allows accounts receivable to be reported by operating segment in compliance with IFRS 8.

Figure 3.34 General Ledger View of a Document with Simulation of Document Splitting

A more detailed example showing the entry view and the general ledger view for a vendor invoice document is as follows. Table 3.11 shows the entry view of a vendor invoice posting to multiple expense accounts,

Note that the three expense accounts have been posted with cost centers that have derived profit centers that with segment reporting active have now derived segments. Table 3.12 shows the general ledger view of the same posting and the impact of document splitting with segment.

Key	Account	Account Description	Amount	Curr.	Cost Center	Profit Center	Segment
31	100000	CAPE vendor	10,000	USD			
40	500000	Consulting	4,000	USD	C1	P1	Pulp
40	500500	Travel	3,500	USD	C2	P2	Paper
40	500900	Meals	2,500	USD	C3	P3	Tissue

Table 3.11 Example of Vendor Invoice Posting: Entry View

Key	Account	Account Description	Amount	Curr.	Cost Center	Profit Center	Segment
31	211000	Accounts payable	4,000	USD		P1	Pulp
31	211000	Accounts payable	3,500	USD		P2	Paper
31	211000	Accounts payable	2,500	USD		P3	Tissue
40	500000	Consulting	4,000	USD	C1	P1	Pulp
40	500500	Travel	3,500	USD	C2	P2	Paper
40	500900	Meals	2,500	USD	C3	P3	Tissue

Table 3.12 Example of Vendor Invoice Posting: General Ledger View

Table 3.12 shows that the vendor lines have been split by segments corresponding to the expense accounts. This again allows total accounts payable to be reported by operating segment in compliance with IFRS 8.

> **Note**
>
> The Cost Center field on the split line items in Table 3.12 is blank. This is because the cost center update scenario was not linked to the leading ledger

This section has explained how to set up document splitting in SAP General Ledger and provided examples to show its benefits for IFRS. The next section will explain foreign currency valuation and translation and how it can generate different valuations for accounting principles such as IFRS, U.S. GAAP, and so on.

3.4.4 Foreign Currency Valuation and Translation

Foreign currency valuation and translation has significantly changed in SAP General Ledger compared to the Classic general ledger. There are new transaction codes and programs for foreign currency valuation and translation, shown in Table 3.13.

	Transaction Code	Program
Foreign currency valuation	FAGL_FC_VAL	FAGL_FC_VALUATION
Foreign currency translation	FAGL_FC_TRANS	FAGL_FC_TRANSLATION

Table 3.13 Transaction Codes and Programs for Foreign Currency Valuation

SAP made many of these changes to comply with IFRS and to have the ability to perform multiple valuations across different ledgers.

Chapter 2 provided an overview of IAS 21, The Effects of Changes in Foreign Exchange Rates; valuation and translation can be defined as follows:

▶ *Foreign currency valuation* is defined as the translation of foreign currency transactions into functional (company code) currency. IAS 21 states that all foreign currency transactions must be translated at the exchange rate on the date of the transaction and then at the end of each reporting period. The exceptions to this are nonmonetary items such as assets, which should remain at historical cost. All exchange differences must be shown in the statement of comprehensive income.

▶ *Foreign currency translation* is defined as the translation of the functional (company code) currency into another presentation currency such as group currency. IAS 21 states that assets and liabilities must be translated using the exchange rate on the closing day of the reporting period, and income and expenses must be translated using the exchange rates at the date of the transactions. All exchange differences must be shown as equity.

This section will cover the customizing for foreign currency valuation and translation in SAP General Ledger and will then provide examples of the postings.

Foreign Currency Valuation and Translation Customizing

Figure 3.35 shows the IMG customizing for foreign currency valuation and translation.

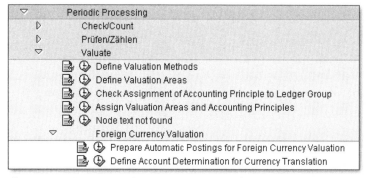

Figure 3.35 Customizing for Foreign Currency Valuation and Translation

The first tasks that apply to both foreign currency valuation and translation are as follows:

- **Define Valuation Methods**

  In this task, you must define valuation methods for how open items will be valuated. To comply with IFRS and specifically IAS 21, you usually need at least two valuation methods, one for valuation and one for translation, as shown in Figure 3.36

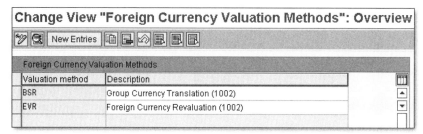

Figure 3.36 Valuation Methods for Revaluation and Translation

Behind each valuation method, you must specify other criteria as shown in Figure 3.37. CAPE Global Consulting recommends using different document types for valuation and translation. In Figure 3.37, for example, the valuation method EVR will post with document type ZA (valuation method BSR is set up with document type ZB). Also, note that the exchange rate used is 1002, which is a period end rate in compliance with IAS 21.

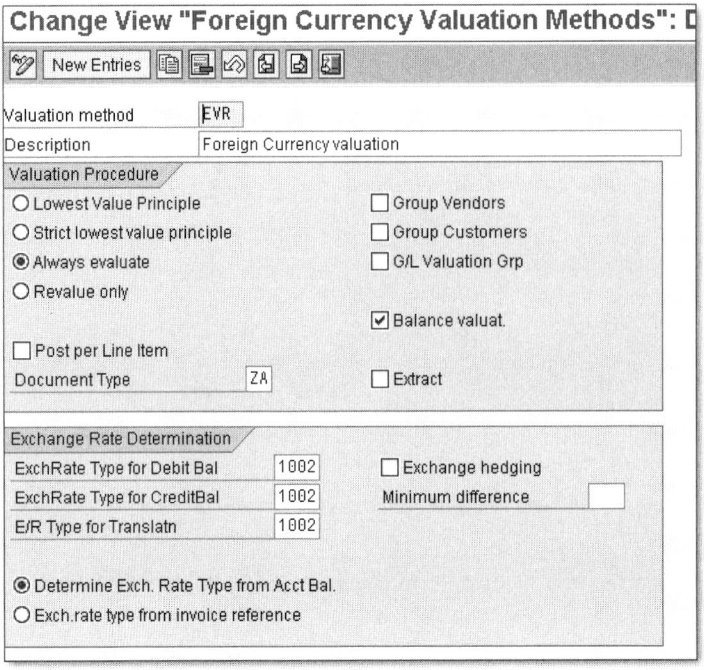

Figure 3.37 Example of a Valuation Method

▶ **Define Valuation Areas**

After the valuation methods have been created, you must create valuation areas and assign them to the valuation methods. Using valuation areas, you can perform different valuations and determine the general ledger accounts that will be posted to. Figure 3.38 shows the valuation methods EVR and BSR assigned to two valuation areas, RV for valuation and GR for translation. In this case, valuation area RV is used to valuate foreign currency transactions to the functional (company code) currency as per IAS 21, so the currency type is company code currency. Valuation area GR is used to translate the functional currency into the presentation (group) currency as per IAS 21, so the currency type is group currency.

Note

One major change in SAP General Ledger for foreign currency customizing is that for translation you must use a financial statement version for account determination. This will be covered in a later section, but as can be seen from Figure 3.38, the valuation area for translation GR is linked to financial statement version JM00.

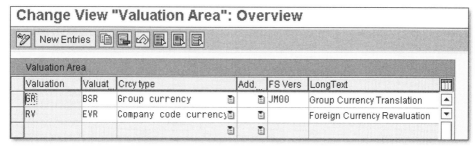

Figure 3.38 Valuation Areas and Assignment to Valuation Methods

▶ **Assign Valuation Areas and Accounting Principles**

In this task you must assign the previously created valuation areas to their respective accounting principles. Figure 3.39 shows that valuation areas RV and GR in this case are both linked to the accounting principle for IFRS. However, for a local GAAP with different foreign currency valuation than IFRS, you would create a different valuation area and assign it to the accounting principle for local GAAP. The parallel ledgers section earlier in this chapter showed how the accounting principles are assigned to their ledgers.

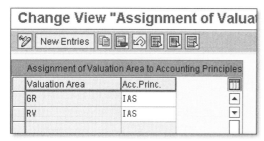

Figure 3.39 Assign Valuation Areas to Accounting Principles

▶ **Prepare Automatic Postings for Foreign Currency Valuation**

In this task, you set up the account determination for the posting of exchange differences resulting from the valuation of foreign currency transactions into the functional currency. Figure 3.40 shows the available transactions.

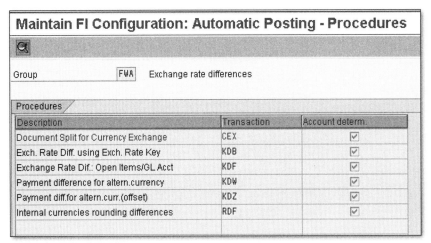

Figure 3.40 Prepare Automatic Postings for Foreign Currency Valuation

The most commonly used transactions that you need to set up in this table are KDB for exchange differences on non-open item managed accounts and KDF for open item managed accounts.

Figure 3.41 shows an example of the setup for KDB. An exchange rate difference key called REVL has been set up to post to general ledger account 711100 in this example, which is in the statement of comprehensive income as per the IAS 21 requirements. Any non-open item managed general ledger accounts that have foreign currency transactions and are monetary items should have this REVL exchange rate difference key added to their master records. An example of this is the confirmed cash account for a foreign currency bank account.

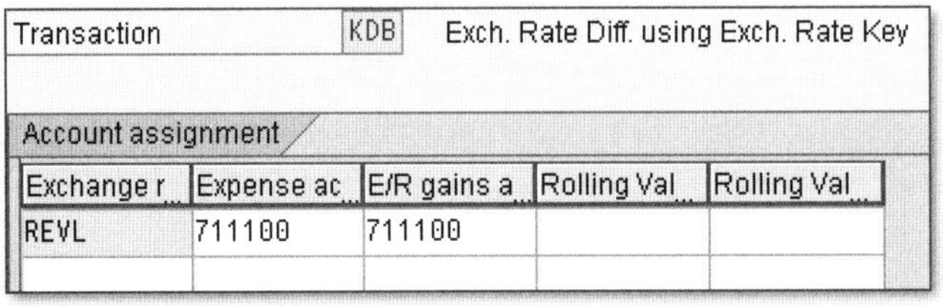

Transaction	KDB	Exch. Rate Diff. using Exch. Rate Key		
Account assignment				
Exchange r	Expense ac	E/R gains a	Rolling Val	Rolling Val
REVL	711100	711100		

Figure 3.41 KDB Transaction for Exchange Differences

Figure 3.42 shows an example of the setup for KDF that is for open item managed accounts.

	G/L Acc	Crcy	Bal.sheet adj.	Loss	Gain
	100113	SEK	100119	711100	711100
	100115	SEK	100119	711100	711100
	100118	SEK	100119	711100	711100

Valuation Area RV

Figure 3.42 KDF Transaction for Exchange Differences

The KDF transaction can be set up by valuation area, so the example shown in Figure 3.42 is for valuation area RV. This table must include all open item managed and reconciliation accounts that have foreign currency transactions and are monetary items. Examples of these include foreign currency bank clearing accounts, accounts receivable, and accounts payable reconciliation accounts.

▶ **Define Account Determination for Currency Translation**

This is new for SAP General Ledger and was not in the Classic general ledger. In this task, you set up the account determination for the posting of exchange differences resulting from the translation of the functional currency transactions into the presentation (group) currency. As shown in Figure 3.38, above, the valuation area for group currency is linked to financial statement version JM00. Figure 3.43 shows the selection screen; you must maintain the account determination for your chart of accounts, valuation area (GR in our example), and financial statement version (JM00 in our example).

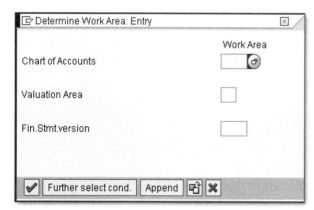

Figure 3.43 Selection Screen for Currency Translation Account Determination

Figure 3.44 shows the account determination table for currency translation. For foreign currency valuation the exchange differences are set to post to the statement of comprehensive income. However, in compliance with IAS 21, the currency translation must be shown in equity, so the exchange differences in this table are set to post to a general ledger equity account (340500 in this example).

Valuation Area	GR					
Fin.Stmt Vers.	JM00					

Account Determination for Translation of Balances						
FS Item	Debit bal. E/R type	Credit bal. E/R type	Bal.sheet adj.	Val.loss 1	Val.gain 1
100010	1002	1002	100999	340500	340500
100013	1002	1002	100999	340500	340500
100015	1002	1002	100999	340500	340500
100018	1002	1002	100999	340500	340500
100020	1002	1002	100999	340500	340500

Figure 3.44 Account Determination for Currency Translation

Note that in the table shown in Figure 3.44, the financial statement (FS) item is used instead of a general ledger account. This means you have to maintain a financial statement version before this table can be maintained. Using a financial statement version instead of general ledger accounts allows you to group accounts that have similar posting for translation exchange differences. Figure 3.45 shows an example of the financial statement version used in this example.

```
JM00 Financial Statement for Currency Translation

    ─── 100010  100010
    ─── 100013  100013
    ─── 100015  100015
    ─── 100018  100018
    ─── 100020  100020
    ─── 100023  100023
    ─── 100025  100025
```

Figure 3.45 Example of Financial Statement Version for Currency Translation

This completes the section on customizing for foreign currency valuation and translation. The next section provides examples of the transactions and their corresponding output.

Foreign Currency Valuation and Translation Transactions

As mentioned previously, the transaction for foreign currency valuation is FAGL_FC_VAL. This has similar selection criteria to the transaction in the Classic general ledger, F.05. Figure 3.46 shows the first screen of the selection criteria for this transaction.

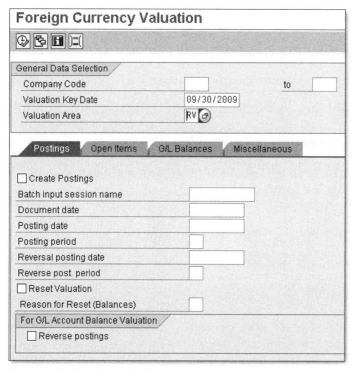

Figure 3.46 First Screen for Foreign Currency Valuation Transaction

As can be seen, this transaction must be run by a valuation key date, which as per IAS 21 is usually the last day of the reporting period, and by valuation area, which should be the valuation area for translating into company code currency, RV in our example. On the G/L Balances tab the exchange rate difference key that was set up for the KDB transaction can be used to select only the general ledger balance accounts that should be valued.

Figure 3.47 shows an example of a posting proposal for Transaction FAGL_FC_VAL. As can be seen, the ledger being posted to is L1. This is because previously, the accounting principle for IFRS was linked to ledger group L1, and then valuation area RV was linked to the accounting principle for IFRS. This demonstrates that you can set up different valuation areas to post to one or more parallel ledgers. Also, note that the offset account in this example is 711100, which was set up under the KDB and KDF transactions. This is an account in the statement of comprehensive income as per IAS 21.

> **Note**
>
> CAPE Global Consulting has found that in practice our U.S. customers use the same valuation areas for both U.S. GAAP and IFRS foreign currency postings because the rules are similar. However, in Latin America, we have customers with different foreign currency valuation for local GAAP, so they need different valuation areas

```
Ledger Group L1 Posting Proposal

Ledger CoCd DocumentNo Document Header Text      Typ Pstng Date Crcy  LCurr LCur2 LCur3 Text
Itm PK G/L            Amount in LC      LC2 amount      LC3 amount Text

L1     1310           FC valuation               09/30/2009 USD   CAD   USD
  1 50 711100         372,869.52        298,295.62                100200 - Valuation on 20090930
  2 40 100200         372,869.52        298,295.62                100200 - Valuation on 20090930

L1     1310           FC valuation               09/30/2009 USD   CAD   USD
  1 50 711100         13,105.49         10,484.39                 100290 - Valuation on 20090930
  2 40 100290         13,105.49         10,484.39                 100290 - Valuation on 20090930

L1     1310           FC valuation               09/30/2009 USD   CAD   USD
  1 50 711100         111.91            89.53                     111101 - Valuation on 20090930
  2 40 111101         111.91            89.53                     111101 - Valuation on 20090930
```

Figure 3.47 Example of Posting Proposal for Foreign Currency Valuation

The transaction for foreign currency translation is FAGL_FC_TRANS. This is a new transaction in SAP General Ledger, and Figure 3.48 shows the selection criteria screen for this transaction.

As can be seen from Figure 3.48, this transaction must also be run by a key date, which is the last day of the reporting period, and by valuation area, which is GR in our example. Under IAS 21 for foreign currency translation, all assets and liabilities are translated (excluding equity). The statement of comprehensive income accounts must be translated at the exchange rate on the date of the transaction.

Note

Many SAP customers have daily exchange rates and so do not need to use the Valuate P&L Accounts and Val.period balance only options in this transaction.

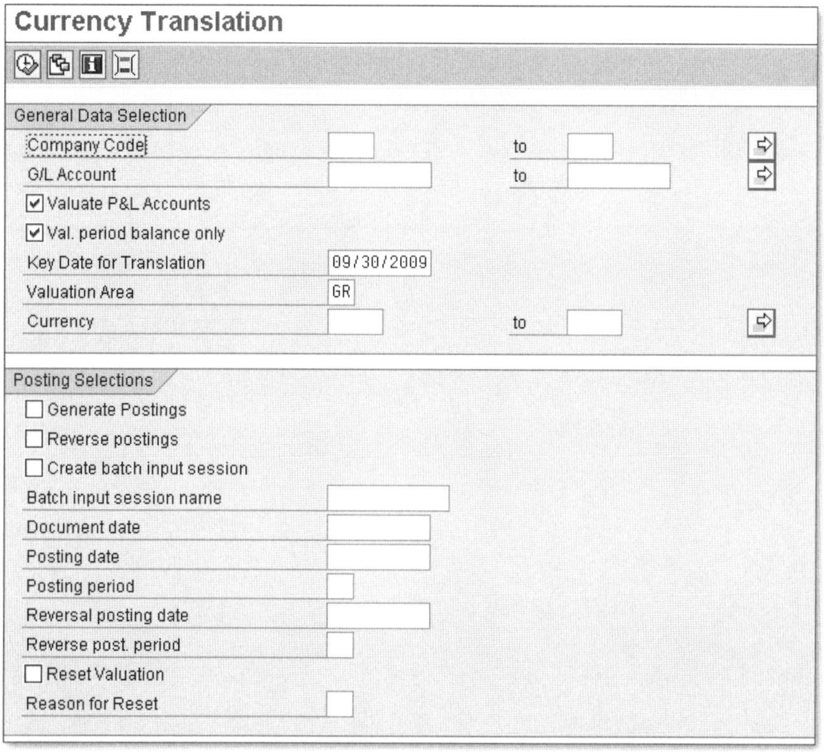

Currency Translation

General Data Selection

Company Code		to	
G/L Account		to	

☑ Valuate P&L Accounts
☑ Val. period balance only
Key Date for Translation 09/30/2009
Valuation Area GR
Currency to

Posting Selections

☐ Generate Postings
☐ Reverse postings
☐ Create batch input session
Batch input session name
Document date
Posting date
Posting period
Reversal posting date
Reverse post. period
☐ Reset Valuation
Reason for Reset

Figure 3.48 Selection Screen for Foreign Currency Translation Transaction

Figure 3.49 shows an example of a posting proposal for Transaction FAGL_FC_TRANS. As can be seen, the ledger being posted to is L1 because previously, the accounting principle for IFRS was linked to ledger group L1, and then valuation area GR was linked to the accounting principle for IFRS. Also, note that the offset account in this example is 340500, which was set up in the account determination for currency translation. This is an equity account in the statement of financial position as per IAS 21.

```
Ledger Group L1 Posting Proposal

CoCd DocumentNo Document Header Text      Typ Pstng Date Crcy  LCurr LCur2 LCur3 Text
Itm PK G/L              Amount in LC       LC2 amount       LC3 amount Text

1310          5  GR20090930000000100200        09/30/2009 USD  CAD   USD
  1 40 340500                0.00       310,978.27                   100200 - Translation per…
  2 50 100200                0.00       310,978.27                   100200 - Translation per…

1310          5  GR20090930000000100290        09/30/2009 USD  CAD   USD
  1 40 340500                0.00        13,558.65                   100290 - Translation per…
  2 50 100290                0.00        13,558.65                   100290 - Translation per…

1310          5  GR20090930000000111101        09/30/2009 USD  CAD   USD
  1 40 340500                0.00            89.53                   111101 - Translation per…
  2 50 111101                0.00            89.53                   111101 - Translation per…
```

Figure 3.49 Example of Posting Proposal for Foreign Currency Translation

This completes the section on the third useful functionality in SAP General Ledger for IFRS. We have covered segment reporting, document splitting, and foreign currency valuation, which many larger companies use for their transition to IFRS. The remainder of this chapter will explain the SAP functionality for IFRS in components other than SAP General Ledger.

3.5   IFRS Functionality in Other SAP Components

There are other SAP components that provide functionality to assist with the transition to IFRS. This section will cover the three main components that impact IFRS. We will start with consolidations.

3.5.1   Consolidations

The recommended solution for planning and consolidation in an SAP system for IFRS is to use products from the SAP BusinessObjects suite. The area of consolidations in SAP systems can be a little confusing to customers because in recent years there have been many choices. Previously, in earlier releases such as SAP R/3, customers used either EC-CS (Enterprise Controlling – Consolidation System) or SAP SEM-BCS (SAP Strategic Enterprise Management – Business Consolidation System).

In 2007, SAP acquired a company called BusinessObjects, which specialized in business consolidation functionality, and SAP now has two consolidation products, SAP BusinessObjects Planning and Consolidation and SAP BusinessObjects Financial Consolidation. This section will focus on SAP BusinessObjects Planning and Consolidation because SAP BusinessObjects Financial Consolidation is generally only used by companies with complex consolidation requirements and does not include planning. SAP BusinessObjects Planning and Consolidation will be the primary consolidation product for SAP in the future, and it is expected that these two applications will be merged in 2010 as part of Financial Performance Management 8.0.

SAP will continue to offer SAP SEM-BCS, but there will be no further enhancements to the product, and it will be in maintenance mode until 2011.

> **Note**
>
> Many of CAPE Global Consulting's customers are using SEM-BCS and ask us whether they should upgrade to SAP BusinessObjects Planning and Consolidation as part of their transition to IFRS. Our answer to this question is that there is not an immediate need to upgrade to SAP BusinessObjects Planning and Consolidation because, for example, SAP BusinessObjects XBRL Publishing by UBmatrix is compatible with both SAP BusinessObjects Planning and Consolidation and SAP SEM-BCS. However, because SAP BusinessObjects Planning and Consolidation will be the primary consolidation product in the future, new installations of SAP systems and existing SAP customers switching from third-party consolidation applications such as Hyperion, must seriously consider this application.

SAP BusinessObjects Planning and Consolidation is an excellent solution for IFRS. Some of its key features and benefits include:

▶ **Single application and user interface**
All planning and consolidation tools are in SAP BusinessObjects Planning and Consolidation; no integration is required between multiple applications.

▶ **Parallel reporting**
SAP BusinessObjects Planning and Consolidation can easily meet the requirements for IFRS and U.S. GAAP during the dual reporting period.

► **Top-side adjustments**
You can make consolidation adjustments directly in SAP BusinessObjects Planning and Consolidation.

► **Disclosures and commentary**
The application enables users to provide detailed disclosure, which is required by IFRS.

► **Improved decision making**
SAP BusinessObjects Planning and Consolidation has flexible and powerful reporting tools.

► **Provision of IFRS starter kits**
These were introduced in July 2009. See below for more information.

► **Comprehensive compliance reducing risk**
SAP BusinessObjects Planning and Consolidation is based on rules that assist with compliance.

► **Integration with SAP ERP 6.0 and SAP General Ledger**
For example, the application integrates with the parallel ledger functionality in SAP General Ledger.

► **Reduced cycle time**
The planning and budgeting process is more efficient.

► **Familiar user interface**
The application can be used easily by Microsoft users, for example, Excel and Web-based environments.

In 2009, SAP introduced an IFRS starter kit, as mentioned above, for consolidations that is preconfigured for IFRS and contains the IFRS rules, IFRS chart of accounts, IFRS financial statement formats, and so on. Although SAP Business-Objects has been used for many years by companies in countries transitioning to IFRS, this starter kit will make the transition easier for countries such as Canada and the U.S. SAP states that the starter kit can reduce implementation times by up to 80% and results in rapid and trusted legal compliance.

> **Note**
>
> To install the IFRS starter kit, you must have already installed SAP BusinessObjects Planning and Consolidation 7.0 and SAP BusinessObjects XBRL Publishing by UBmatrix (see next section).

Table 3.14 shows a sample of some of the financial statement predefined formats included in the starter kit.

Code	Description
C1	**Annual report**
C11	**Financial statements**
C11-05	Statement of financial position
C11-10	Income statement
C11-15	Statement of other comprehensive income
C11-20	Statement of comprehensive income
C11-25	Statement of cash flows
C11-30	Statement of changes in equity
C12	**Financial statements by segment**
C12-05	Revenue by segment
C12-20	Revenue by geographical area
C12-25	Non-current assets by geographical area

Table 3.14 Sample of Reports in the IFRS Starter Kit

Many SAP customers still use a manual process for their consolidation, for example, spreadsheets. CAPE Global Consulting offers a service to migrate an existing consolidation solution to SAP BusinessObjects Planning and Consolidation. This service starts with an assessment of your existing planning and consolidation solution, and we then provide a roadmap for how to migrate to SAP BusinessObjects Planning and Consolidation. We also provide recommendations for how to use the application most effectively for IFRS.

SAP BusinessObjects Planning and Consolidation functionality for consolidations is excellent for producing consolidated financial statements that meet IFRS requirements. Many of the IFRS requirements discussed in Chapter 2, such as how to account for business combinations, can easily be addressed in this application.

Many European companies have successfully used SAP BusinessObjects Planning and Consolidation during their transition to IFRS, and the recent addition of the IFRS starter kit will help reduce the transition time.

This section has introduced the consolidation functionality available from SAP for IFRS. The next section will discuss the functionality for reporting the consolidated results by XBRL.

Note

For more detail on SAP BusinessObjects Planning and Consolidation, please refer to an upcoming SAP Press book, *SAP Business Planning & Consolidation*, by Muthu Ranganathan, which is scheduled for release in January 2010.

3.5.2   XBRL

The eXtensible Business Reporting Language (XBRL) has become the global standard for exchanging financial information. It is already required in Europe and many other countries, and it was recently made mandatory for listed U.S. companies starting with fiscal years ending on or after June 15, 2009. It will be a phased requirement over three years for the U.S. as follows:

▶ The largest (market value $5 billion or higher) listed U.S. companies must report with XBRL starting in 2009

▶ Listed U.S. companies using accelerated filing in 2010

▶ All remaining listed U.S. companies in 2011

Some of the features of XBRL are the following:

▶ Each jurisdiction defines its own *taxonomy*. This is a set of agreed upon, computer-readable tags for individual data items in financial statements and how they interrelate.

▶ It provides easier to compare financial information between companies.

▶ It is easier to search and analyze financial information owing to tagging.

The recommended SAP solution for XBRL is to use SAP BusinessObjects XBRL Publishing application by UBmatrix. Figure 3.50 shows the relationship between SAP BusinessObjects Planning and Consolidation and XBRL by UBmatrix.

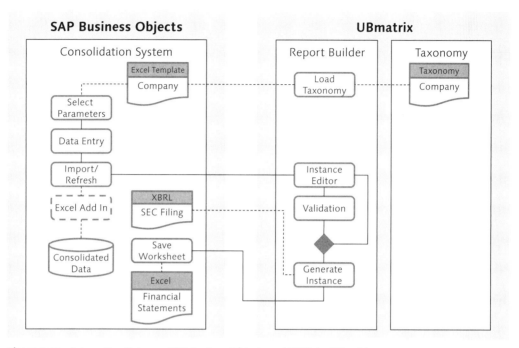

Figure 3.50 Integration Between SAP BusinessObjects and XBRL by UBmatrix

SAP states that the three main benefits from using this application instead of outsourcing your XBRL publishing are as follows:

1. **Speed**

   ▶ Fast navigation of taxonomies and mapping of data

   ▶ Easy to use drag-and drop mapping environment

   ▶ Fast, thorough validation of generated XBRL documents

2. **Simplicity**

   ▶ Works with Enterprise Performance Management (EPM) and SAP Business Suite.

   ▶ Links to and can import disclosures from Microsoft Word.

   ▶ Users do not deal with complex XBRL syntax.

3. **Flexibility**

   ▶ XBRL taxonomies can be easily extended.

▶ Complies with XBRL 2.1 specification.

▶ Supports basic and block-text footnotes, dimensions, and business rules.

The SAP BusinessObjects XBRL application can work with SAP consolidation applications such as:

▶ SAP BusinessObjects Planning and Consolidation (see Figure 3.51)

▶ SAP BusinessObjects Financial Consolidation

▶ SAP SEM-BCS (see Figure 3.52)

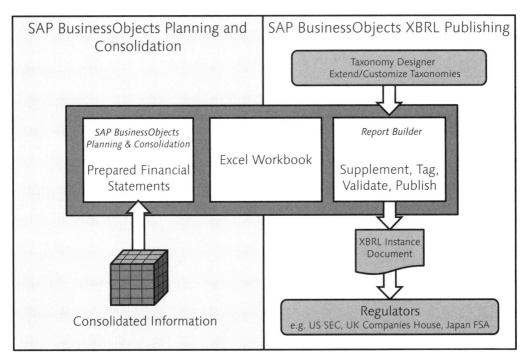

Figure 3.51 Integration Between SAP BusinessObjects Planning and Consolidation and XBRL Publishing by UBmatrix

It can also work with data from any non-SAP consolidation application or other business software and tags, transforms, and maps data to produce XBRL documents quickly and accurately.

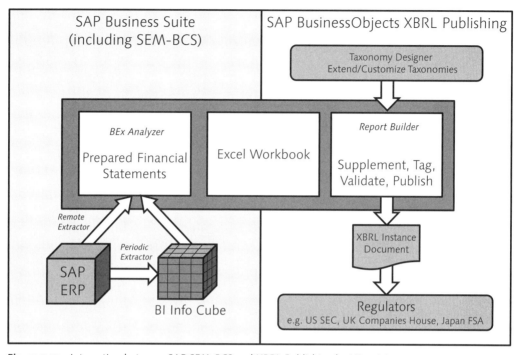

Figure 3.52 Integration between SAP SEM-BCS and XBRL Publishing by UBmatrix

A main benefit of using the SAP BusinessObjects XBRL Publishing application is that you can be sure that the generated XBRL documents are correct for your chosen taxonomy.

Although XBRL publishing is separate from IFRS because other GAAPs can also be published in XBRL, many people feel that the adoption of XBRL in the U.S. will help with the transition to IFRS in the U.S.

Note

CAPE Global Consulting recommends that customers decide how XBRL will be generated early in their transition to IFRS. The SAP BusinessObjects XBRL Publishing application is an excellent tool, is easy to use, and in our experience requires less maintenance than alternative solutions.

3.5.3   Asset Accounting

The Asset Accounting (FI-AA) component provides excellent functionality for parallel reporting, but it is extremely important that the depreciation areas are set up correctly, especially when you are using the parallel ledger solution.

Section 3.3 described the parallel reporting options for IFRS, and the various options showed the FI-AA depreciation area 01 either set to a local GAAP (such as U.S. GAAP) or IFRS. When you use the parallel ledger approach, the depreciation area 01 must be set to the same accounting principle as the leading ledger 0L. So, for example, if you are using the leading ledger for IFRS, the FI-AA depreciation area 01 must also be set to IFRS.

Figure 3.53 shows an example of the setup of asset depreciation areas for one of our Latin American IFRS projects. As can be seen, the FI-AA depreciation area 01 is linked to the leading ledger 0L, which is IFRS, and two other depreciation areas, 02 and 03, are linked to two parallel ledgers L1 and L2.

> **Note**
>
> A depreciation area change can only be accomplished by an SAP SLO service.

Ár.	Denominación del área de valoración	Real	Lib.mayor	Gr.dest.
	Caracterizar áreas de valoración			
1	Area según norma IFRS	☑	1	0L
2	Area según norma tributaria	☑	3	L2
3	Area según norma local	☑	3	L1
4	Area Corporativa sin Revalorización	☑	0	
5	Area según norma local en USD	☑	0	
6	Area según norma IFRS en USD	☑	0	
7	Area Tributaria dolar	☑	0	
20	Revaluación IFRS	☑	0	
21	Revaluación IFRS - USD	☑	0	
22	Combinación Negocios	☑	0	
23	Combinación Negocios USD	☑	0	
24	Deterioro	☑	0	
25	Deterioro USD	☑	0	
50	Delta 02-01	☐	6	L2
51	Delta 03-01	☐	6	L1
52	DELTA 05-06	☐	0	
53	DELTA 07-06	☐	0	

Figure 3.53   Asset Depreciation Areas Linked to Parallel Ledgers

3.5.4   Other Functionality

SAP continues to add functionality to other components that facilitates the transition to IFRS. An example of this is in the material ledger, where inventory is depreciated using the local depreciation method and there is no way at present to use a parallel valuation and depreciate using a different depreciation method such as for IFRS.

SAP is in the process of developing new material ledger functionality for this parallel valuation of inventory that will be included in Enhancement Package 5. It will allow the mapping of a second depreciation method to a second version in the CO component that is only used for parallel valuation of inventories.

This is just an example of how SAP is meeting companies' requirements as they transition to IFRS.

3.6   Summary

The purpose of this chapter was to introduce the functionality in SAP ERP Financials that will be most used in the transition to IFRS. Obviously, parallel reporting is one of the main issues, especially with countries such as the U.S. requiring a dual reporting period. Also, even in countries where IFRS is adopted immediately such as in Chile, many companies still require their local GAAP such as Chilean GAAP for tax reporting.

Therefore, this chapter described the two solutions in SAP ERP Financials for parallel reporting, which are parallel accounts and parallel ledgers. Parallel accounts can also be used in the Classic general ledger, but the use of parallel ledgers in SAP General Ledger is usually a better solution, especially for larger companies.

Section 3.3 described the options for IFRS, depending on whether parallel accounts or parallel ledgers are used. The recommendations differ for companies that are already using SAP compared to those that will be undertaking a new installation of SAP.

The chapter then described other useful functionality in SAP General Ledger and focused on segment reporting, document splitting, and foreign currency valuation.

It described the use of this functionality and how to set it up for IFRS. Most customers of CAPE Global Consulting have set up document splitting with segments to produce fully balanced financial statements by segment.

Finally, the chapter explained IFRS functionality in other components such as SAP BusinessObjects Planning and Consolidation and SAP BusinessObjects XBRL Publishing. The combination of SAP General Ledger with SAPs consolidation and XBRL applications delivers an efficient, streamlined, and flexible solution to assist with your transition to IFRS.

Whereas this chapter focused on SAP functionality for IFRS, the next chapter will explain the technology changes that are required to use SAP ERP 6.0 and SAP General Ledger. It will start with an overview of upgrading to SAP ERP 6.0 and then migrating to SAP General Ledger. It will also discuss new migration scenarios designed for companies that are already using SAP General Ledger but need to add functionality for IFRS such as document splitting or parallel ledgers.

This chapter will explain the technical changes that are required for your IFRS project if you want to use the latest SAP functionality in SAP General Ledger.

4 SAP Upgrade and General Ledger Migrations

4.1 Introduction

To use SAP General Ledger there are only two options available:

1. A new installation of SAP

2. An upgrade to SAP ERP and then a migration project

This chapter will explain the upgrade and migration. Upgrading to SAP ERP is a prerequisite for migrating to SAP General Ledger. Section 4.2 will explain the upgrade to SAP ERP 6.0, and Section 4.3 will explain the migration scenarios for migrating from the Classic general ledger to the new SAP General Ledger. The chapter will conclude with Section 4.4, which will explain the new migration scenarios for companies that already use SAP General Ledger but need to add new functionality in preparation for their transition to IFRS.

4.2 Upgrade to SAP ERP 6.0

We recommend separate projects for the SAP ERP upgrade and the SAP General Ledger migration. Both are highly complex projects, and keeping them separate increases the likelihood of success for both.

SAP ERP 6.0 (SAP ERP) is the latest release from SAP, and it offers improved functionality for financial management, human capital management, procurement and logistics, product development and manufacturing, sales and service, and other corporate services. SAP ERP is powered by the SAP NetWeaver platform, which offers several benefits that we will explain in Section 4.2.1.

This section will detail the benefits of upgrading to SAP ERP, explain the three upgrade approaches and the future release strategy, and finally, describe best practices for running an upgrade project.

SAP ERP is based on a single platform called SAP NetWeaver, and all of the components of SAP ERP reside on this single platform. Industry solutions, for example, are now offered within the core of SAP ERP. There are also technical benefits of using the SAP NetWeaver platform and other functional benefits, as we'll describe in the next section.

4.2.1 Benefits of Upgrading

The aim of SAP ERP is to provide a solid business foundation that enables companies to meet today's business challenges. General benefits of SAP ERP over SAP R/3 include flexibility, business risk mitigation, and business process improvement.

Benefits of SAP NetWeaver

SAP ERP is based on a business platform called SAP NetWeaver. The benefits of this platform are as follows:

▶ SAP NetWeaver unifies into a single platform all technology components that are needed to run SAP ERP. This results in a reduction of IT costs and the ability to rapidly deploy additional SAP and third-party products.

▶ Enterprise service-oriented architecture (SOA) allows greater flexibility and business integration.

▶ Enhanced search capabilities and the integration of analytical functions through SAP NetWeaver Business Warehouse (BW) components are a clear advancement. SAP NetWeaver allows users to access a range of enterprise-wide analytics leading to improved decision making. This supports improved workforce productivity; SAP ERP presents information in an integrated view, enabling tasks and analytics to be completed faster.

► As the foundation for SOA, SAP NetWeaver helps align people, information, and business processes across the entire organization.

Functional Benefits

SAP ERP provides many functional enhancements. These and other benefits to an organization include:

► **New functionality and improvements of existing processes**
   Major improvements have been made in SAP ERP Financials, for example, SAP General Ledger, and in many other components such as corporate performance management (as shown in Figure 4.1). Figure 4.1 also shows some of the enhancements in business planning, business consolidation, and performance measurement.

► **Improved employee productivity**
   SAP ERP presents information in an integrated view, enabling tasks to be completed faster and better decisions to be made.

► **Reduction of IT costs**
   With the new functionality provided in SAP ERP, many user modifications implemented in previous releases, such as SAP R/3, can now be replaced by SAP standard functions. Also, SOA allows for lower-risk upgrades.

► **Increased compliance**
   SAP ERP provides timely and accurate financial reporting and corporate compliance. With the increased corporate governance requirements (e.g., Sarbanes–Oxley and Basel II compliance), SAP ERP provides internal and external audit process with new functionality for the management of internal controls.

► **SAP industry solutions compatibility**
   SAP ERP has more than 25 industry solutions, and there is a deeper level of process integration.

► **Improved reporting and analytics**
   Major improvements have been made to enterprise reporting capabilities including better executive dashboards to aid executive decision making.

► **Easier budgeting and planning processes**
   SAP ERP uses an *express planning* technique to assist users in the construction of budgets and periodic forecasts. This is a far less technical process than in previous SAP releases, so all levels of management can use it.

▶ **Similar user interface**

Another significant benefit of upgrading to SAP ERP from SAP R/3 4.6C or SAP Enterprise is that the new interface is similar to the previous one. This results in little end user training and therefore minimal disruption to users. Also, any automated testing tools used in previous implementations can be reused with only minor rework.

Benefits of Upgrading from Legacy Systems

In addition to the benefits described so far, there are also benefits of upgrading from outdated legacy systems, especially those with significant user modifications. Problems with existing legacy systems may include:

▶ Outdated client server architecture requiring expensive maintenance and inability to accommodate future growth and changing requirements

▶ Nonintegrated systems preventing timely forecasting and reporting

▶ Multiple instances and disparate systems resulting in incompatibility, unnecessary system redundancy, and lack of organizational visibility

▶ Insufficient financial reporting for current corporate governance and compliance requirements

Finance Benefits

In addition to SAP General Ledger, other new functionalities in SAP ERP Financials will greatly benefit a finance organization. The enhanced financial management, analysis, and reporting functionality in SAP ERP Financials can be highlighted as follows:

▶ New SAP General Ledger that requires fewer manual reconciliations and provides the ability to produce balanced financial statements by multiple dimensions

▶ Improved management dashboards that provide all management information required for better decision making

▶ Business intelligence (BI) functionality that provides the ability to design reports in third-party applications such as Microsoft and to publish reports in third-party formats such as Acrobat documents

- New collections and credit management tools to assist with faster cash collections and improved days sales outstanding

- Single solution for financial capital management (SAP FSCM)

- Improved consolidated financial reporting, which includes functionality for users to consolidate financial information from third-party applications and enhancements for intercompany eliminations and foreign currency valuation

- Improved audit information system (AIS). AIS now supports internal and external audits including activities such as document tracing, account analyses and individual inquiries.

> **Note**
>
> In collaboration with SAP ERP's data retention tool (DART), AIS allows auditors to access several years of data, including data that is not part of financial accounting.

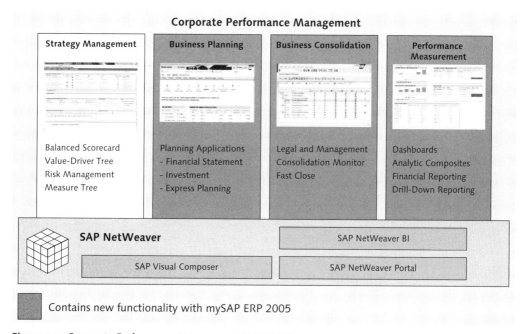

Figure 4.1 Corporate Performance Management in SAP ERP

Now that we have discussed the benefits of SAP ERP and the reasons for upgrading, the next section will discuss the three approaches to upgrading.

4.2.2 Upgrade Approaches

Customers need to determine their main reasons for upgrading and the business improvements that they expect from the upgrade. This helps determine the upgrade approach because there are three different approaches, which will be explained in this section. The approach chosen depends on the reason for upgrading, expected return on investment (ROI), and payback. An overview of the three approaches followed by a detailed description is as follows:

- **Technical upgrade**
  The focus of a technical upgrade is on maintaining an existing solution. No new functionality is added or system modifications are removed.

- **Functional upgrade**
  The focus of a functional upgrade is on using the new functionality in SAP ERP to remove custom modifications in the existing system.

- **Strategic business improvement upgrade**
  The focus of a strategic business improvement upgrade is on improving the existing solution by not only removing modifications but also reengineering business processes. Implementation of additional applications may be included in this upgrade, for example, implementing a new component such as travel management, which was not in the existing solution.

Figure 4.2 displays the three upgrade approaches graphically, showing their relationship with the initial level of modification of the system being upgraded. For example, if the current system is highly modified and a technical upgrade is performed, there is no change to the level of system modification.

For the transition to IFRS, the majority of companies start with a technical upgrade, which upgrades them to SAP ERP with less preparation required than the other two approaches and with the lowest risk. This then allows a company to migrate to SAP General Ledger, and a separate project can then be run at a later date to remove modifications or add new functionality or components.

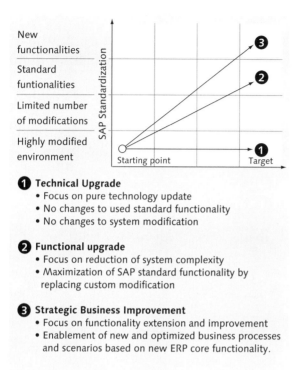

New functionalities

Standard funtionalities

Limited number of modifications

Highly modified environment

SAP Standardization

Starting point   Target

❶ Technical Upgrade
- Focus on pure technology update
- No changes to used standard functionality
- No changes to system modification

❷ Functional upgrade
- Focus on reduction of system complexity
- Maximization of SAP standard functionality by replacing custom modification

❸ Strategic Business Improvement
- Focus on functionality extension and improvement
- Enablement of new and optimized business processes and scenarios based on new ERP core functionality.

Figure 4.2   Possible Upgrade Approaches

Technical Upgrade

A technical upgrade is an upgrade to the system landscape only. The functionality and degree of complexity in the existing SAP R/3 solution remains exactly the same when you perform a technical upgrade. SAP's current surveys confirm that more than 70% of SAP R/3 customers who have upgraded begin with the technical upgrade. They then consider in a subsequent step the opportunities to add the new functionality of SAP ERP.

A technical upgrade is the fastest way to upgrade, and it minimizes disruption to the business. Many customers choose this approach to upgrade when they want to utilize the new system landscape of SAP ERP but do not have the resources to undertake a functional upgrade. This upgrade approach focuses on risk mitigation and sustainability of the existing SAP solution. No benefits are obtained from the new functionality available in SAP ERP, although the new functionality can be implemented at a later date.

SAP estimates that on average, a technical upgrade from SAP R/3 to SAP ERP takes three-and-a-half months. The more modifications there are in the existing system, the longer the upgrade will take.

> **Note**
>
> For countries such as Canada that have a deadline of 2011 for IFRS, companies that want to use SAP General Ledger have little choice other than to perform a technical upgrade followed by a migration to SAP General Ledger

Functional Upgrade

A functional upgrade also upgrades the system landscape to SAP ERP but aims to streamline SAP functionality by removing as many modifications as possible from the existing SAP solution and replacing them with new functionality in SAP ERP. SAP estimates that 30% of total upgrade time is spent updating custom code to get it to work in the new SAP ERP software. Significant cost reductions can be made in removing custom code that is no longer required or in cases where the new functionality in SAP ERP makes the custom code obsolete.

In many cases customers have written custom code even when the functionality was available in their SAP release. This may have been due to bad consulting advice, but a functional upgrade presents an excellent opportunity to clean up the system, removing these unnecessary modifications and returning the system to SAP standard wherever possible.

When custom code is still required, a significant amount of time is spent testing the code in SAP ERP. The code will have been written in SAP R/3 using older versions of the ABAP programming language and will not necessarily work the same way in SAP ERP. Therefore, the first step in a functional upgrade is to check the modifications in the SAP R/3 system and compare them with the new functionalities provided by SAP ERP.

Strategic Business Improvement Upgrade

A strategic business improvement upgrade builds on a functional upgrade by evaluating business processes and implementing new SAP ERP functionality where appropriate. In many cases, customers may have implemented an earlier release of SAP software when the functionality in a particular component was insufficient for their needs.

For example, imagine a customer who has a third-party treasury solution and a customer who has a third-party consolidation system. In recent years, SAP functionality has improved greatly in these two areas, and even more so in SAP ERP, so a strategic business improvement upgrade is the time to evaluate the original decisions to use third-party software. Doing so may have been correct at the time, but now these systems can be replaced by SAP software. This lowers costs and improves integration.

> **Note**
>
> As stated previously, it is recommended that most customers start with a technical upgrade. However, SAP reports that 70% of customers that start with a technical upgrade later expand the upgrade into either a functional or strategic business improvement upgrade.

4.2.3 SAP Future Release Strategy

Upgrading to SAP ERP provides long-term planning security with a stable platform because SAP has committed to a new release strategy. Instead of new SAP ERP releases, SAP ERP will follow a five-year cycle, and new functionality will be delivered in *SAP Enhancement Packages*.

The implementation of enhancement packages will be optional, depending on customers' needs. The packages will be cumulative, so the enhancements in Package 1, for example, will also be in Package2. This means customers can implement the latest enhancement package and be up to date.

The current SAP ERP release will receive mainstream maintenance until March 2012. Maintenance details for other SAP R/3 releases are as follows:

▶ **SAP R/3 Enterprise**
Mainstream maintenance until March 2009; extended maintenance from April 2009 to March 2012

▶ **SAP R/3 4.6C**
Mainstream maintenance expired; extended maintenance until December 2009

Planning for an SAP ERP upgrade for the transition to IFRS should start as soon as possible, and it is recommended that you upgrade to the latest SAP ERP release.

4.3   Migrating to SAP General Ledger from the Classic General Ledger

When you have completed your upgrade to SAP ERP, it is then possible to migrate to SAP General Ledger to be able to utilize the functionality explained previously for IFRS such as parallel ledgers, segment reporting, document splitting, and foreign currency valuation. This section will introduce the SAP migration service and the three phases of a migration project, which are planning, migration, and testing and go-live. At present, there are five migration scenarios for migrating from the Classic general ledger, which we will also cover in this section, and three migration scenarios for adding functionality to SAP General Ledger, which we will cover in Section 4.4.

> **Note**
>
> The objective of this section is to introduce some of the key migration areas such as the SAP migration service, migration scenarios, and the migration cockpit. For a more detailed explanation and a step-by-step guide to how to execute the tasks in the migration cockpit please refer to my other book published by SAP PRESS, *Migrate Successfully to the SAP General Ledger*. This book contains a case study of one of CAPE Global Consulting's successful migration projects

4.3.1   SAP Migration Service

SAP requires the use of the SAP migration service for all migrations. It is mandatory, and without signing up for the service you cannot install the migration cockpit, which is essential for the migration. SAP's aim is to provide assistance during the migration project and to help ensure a smooth transition from the Classic general ledger to the SAP General Ledger. Because the purchase of this service is required, communication with SAP should start as early as possible, preferably in the planning phase or before.

SAP provides the migration service for the following reasons:

▸ Accounting is a sensitive area, and maintaining data integrity is essential. The general ledger is the basis for a company's statutory reporting, and company executives are now required to sign off on financial reports, so data must be transferred to the SAP General Ledger correctly.

▸ The migration performs fundamental changes to the database, which increases risk. This is especially true when document splitting is included in the target migration scenario because even data from the prior fiscal year must be enriched with additional account assignments before being transferred to the SAP General Ledger.

▸ Many customers have unique situations that require expert assistance. At present, the SAP migration service offers templates for five target migration scenarios for migrating from the Classic general ledger. Most companies have unique situations and require external consulting to help them adapt the delivered target migration scenarios to meet their own needs.

There are many existing business situations and target scenarios for migration from the Classic general ledger to the SAP General Ledger.

The SAP General Ledger offers new reporting functionalities that differ from the Classic general ledger. For example, many of the standard general ledger reports in the SAP General Ledger now include new fields, such as segment and ledger.

To initiate the SAP migration service you must either contact your SAP account manager or email *newglmigration@sap.com*. The first step is then to complete the SAP questionnaire.

SAP Questionnaire

The purpose of the SAP migration service is for SAP to provide scenario-based migration functionality and guidance combined with service sessions to check data consistency. As shown in Figure 4.3, the migration service is initiated by the customer in the form of a request. This is followed by SAP sending a questionnaire to the customer to obtain information on the forthcoming migration. The questionnaire is a very important part of the planning phase because it helps you assess your initial scenario and decide what the target migration scenario will be.

The questions in the questionnaire are different for migration scenarios 1-5 as opposed to migration scenarios 6-8 (see Section 4.4.1). Both questionnaires can be downloaded from *http://service.sap.com/GLMIG*.

On receipt of the questionnaire, SAP conducts feedback sessions with the customer until they have all of the information required to be able to deliver a fixed-price quote for their migration service.

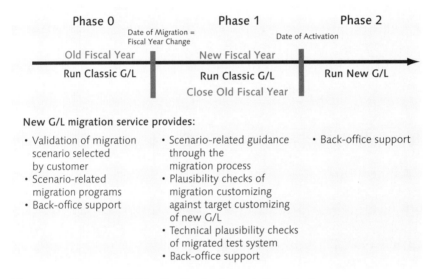

Figure 4.3 How the SAP Migration Service Supports the Project

Service Sessions

Following is a breakdown of the various service sessions.

Service Session 1: Scenario Validation

The main purpose of the first service session is to ensure that the correct migration scenario is being used and for SAP to conduct system analysis in the form of data checks. The data checks are usually conducted in the production system. A sample of the checks is as follows:

▶ That the system is at the required support package level

▶ That the SAP General Ledger is inactive at the client and company code level

▶ Currencies (numbers and consistencies)

▶ Controlling areas (for example, when segmentation is to be implemented)

▶ Financial-specific data checks including:

  ▶ Transaction data records in tables GLT0, GLFUNCT, GLT3, and others

  ▶ Balance sheet adjustment (SAPF180)

  ▶ Cross-company postings

  ▶ Documents and line items (document types, required accounts, etc.)

  ▶ Asset accounting

  ▶ Whether special ledgers are active

The first service session (see Figure 4.4) takes place during phase 0, the planning phase, and SAP delivers a scenario validation report detailing any data cleanup to be performed before the migration.

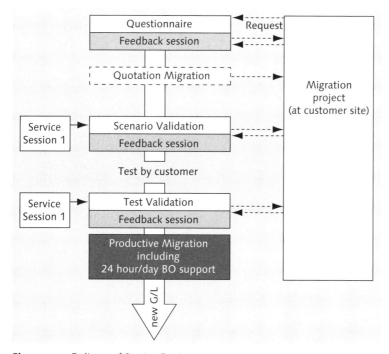

Figure 4.4 Delivery of Service Sessions

Service Session 2: Test Validation

The main purpose of the second service session is to ensure that the test migration was consistent from a technical point of view. Checks during this service session include:

▶ As in service session 1, checking that the system is at the required support package level

▶ Checking the system landscape (productive systems, productive clients, etc.)

▶ Checking components in use (for example, FI-CA)

▶ Migration-scenario-specific checks, such as checking that the periodic postings in asset accounting conform to the migration scenario

▶ Analysis of migration job logs and control tables. For example, checking any manual changes of status by the customer

The second service session takes place in phase 1 (see Figure 4.4), the migration and testing phase, and is performed in the test system. For migrations with a date of migration of January 1, the test validation usually takes place in February or March, and SAP delivers a test validation report detailing any problems found with the test validation.

4.3.2 Migration Scenarios

Five target migration scenarios are covered by the SAP migration service for migrating from the Classic general ledger as shown in Table 4.1.

Scenario	Contents	Benefits
1 — Merge of FI ledger	Merging of the Classic general ledger, consolidation preparation ledger, and cost-of-sales ledger	Reduced data redundancy Faster period-end closing Harmonized reporting
2 — Merge of FI, PCA, and/or Special Purpose Ledger	Scenario 1 and additional merging of Profit Center Accounting and Special Purpose Ledger	Replacement of SPL by the new general ledger Enhanced auditability Better integrated reporting

Table 4.1 Five Target Migration Scenarios Offered by SAP Migration Service for Migrating from Classic General Ledger

Scenario	Contents	Benefits
3 — Merge of FI, PCA, and/ or Special Purpose Ledger plus document splitting	Scenario 2 plus document splitting by, for example, profit center, segment, or business area	Flexible reporting at lower level than company code
4 — Merge of FI, PCA, and/ or Special Purpose Ledger plus parallel ledgers	Scenario 2 plus switch from parallel accounts solution in the Classic general ledger to parallel ledgers solution in the new general ledger	Separation of ledgers gives separate transparency (e.g., for auditors) Can maintain a separate ledger for each accounting principle Fewer general ledger accounts
5 — Merge of FI, PCA, and/ or Special Purpose Ledger plus document splitting plus parallel ledgers	Scenario 3 plus switch from parallel accounts solution in the Classic general ledger to parallel ledgers solution in the new general ledger	Same benefits as in scenarios 3 and 4

Table 4.1 Five Target Migration Scenarios Offered by SAP Migration Service for Migrating from Classic General Ledger (Cont.)

The scenarios range in complexity from scenarios 1 to 5, with 5 being the most complex because it contains both document splitting and parallel ledgers. The time required for a migration project depends on the target migration scenario selected. An estimate of the time required for a migration project is between five and nine months. There are other variables to consider, such as the quality of existing data, system landscape, and so on, but in general, scenario 1 takes approximately five months and scenario 5, seven to nine months.

It should be noted that not all customers find a target migration scenario in Table 4.1 that exactly fits their needs. In this case they must select the scenario that is the best fit. An example of this is a company that currently uses the company code solution for parallel valuation in the Classic general ledger. They now want to migrate to the new general ledger and use the parallel ledgers solution with document splitting for IFRS purposes. In this case they should base their migration on scenario 3 with additional consulting to help make any changes necessary.

> **Note**
>
> CAPE Global Consulting offers a premigration review service. This detailed service provides recommendations for your future migration project including timing, staffing, and possible target migration scenarios. It also highlights current areas that should be worked on or cleaned up in preparation for your project and includes an overview of the new functionality in the SAP General Ledger such as document splitting and parallel ledgers.

Depending on the target migration scenario selected, the SAP migration service provides a very useful tool for managing the activities within the scenario — the general ledger migration cockpit.

4.3.3 Migration Cockpit

The general ledger migration cockpit assists you in managing the three phases of the migration project. The cockpit contains a process tree on the left-hand side and a status monitor on the right-hand side. This tool enables project management to see the tasks that have been completed and the tasks that are still remaining. It is an excellent way for management to quickly see how the migration project is progressing.

Installation of the Migration Cockpit

The first task is to install the general ledger migration cockpit in systems where migrations will take place. This is usually the test migration system and the production system.

There are OSS notes that provide technical information for installing the migration cockpit. The following notes should be consulted:

Number	Short Text
1138250	NMI_CONT: Information about Support Packages
1041066	Installation of NMI Content 2006_1

When the cockpit has been installed, you can access the cockpit with Transaction code CNV_MBT_NGLM, which displays the screen shown in Figure 4.5.

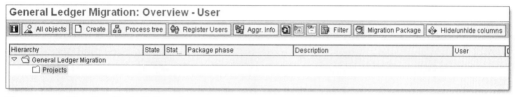

Figure 4.5 Migration Cockpit Overview

The first step is to create your migration project. Clicking once on Projects and then on the Create button brings up the screen shown in Figure 4.6.

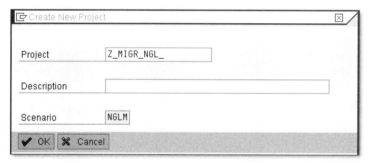

Figure 4.6 Create New Project in Migration Cockpit

In the Project field, enter ⌷ + a code for your project and then enter a full description in the Description field. Click on OK when you are done and you have set up your migration project in the general ledger migration cockpit.

The next step is to load the migration package corresponding to your migration scenario.

Loading the Migration Cockpit Packages

The scenario validation report from SAP confirms the target migration scenario. The most common migration scenarios in our experience for transitions to IFRS have been scenario 3 with document splitting and migration and scenario 5 with document splitting and conversion from parallel accounts to parallel ledgers.

You must now load the migration package for your migration scenario. The following example shows the package for migration scenario 3 being loaded into our previously created migration project. The first step is to click on the project name, that is, ZTEST in this example, and then the Create button. The screen is be similar to Figure 4.7.

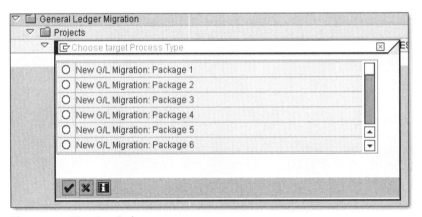

Figure 4.7 Migration Packages

Select the required package and then click on the checkmark icon and the screen will display a pop-up window as in Figure 4.8. This prompts you for an access key that SAP will have provided after you paid for the SAP migration service.

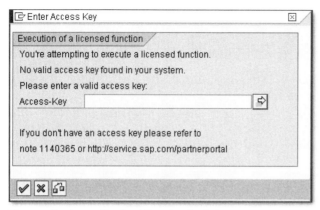

Figure 4.8 Access Key for Migration Cockpit

Enter the access key and click on the checkmark icon. Please note that if you paid for migration scenario 3, the access key will not permit you to load higher packages such as migration scenarios 4 and 5. You can, however, load packages 1 and 2.

Having loaded the package, you next see a screen similar to Figure 4.9. You can either double-click on a package or click once on the package and then on the Process Tree button. This displays a screen similar to Figure 4.10.

General Ledger Migration: Overview

My settings | Create | Process tree | Register Users | Aggr. Info | Filter | Migration Package

Hierarchy	State	Stat	Package phase	Description	Date and time	Process type
▽ ☐ General Ledger Migrati						
▽ ☐ Projects						
▽ ☐ Z_MIGR_NGL_				Migration to New ...	02.12.2008 12:37...	NGLM
▽ ☐ Packages						
90001	☐	🚚	Checkup Phase	New G/L Migration...	02.12.2008 12:42...	New G/L Migration: Package 3
90002	☐	🚚	Setup Phase	New G/L Migration...	02.12.2008 17:01...	New G/L Migration: Package 3
90003	☐	🚚	Setup Phase	New G/L Migration...	19.12.2008 09:55...	New G/L Migration: Package 3

Figure 4.9 Migration Packages Loaded into Migration Project

Process Tree	State	Progress	Tasks	Note	Attachment	Start date	Start time	End date	End time	Run time	Job name
▽ 🌐 90004_TREE_STRUCTURE_HEAD											
▷ ▶ Setup Phase	🚚		📄			05.01.2009	11:07:00			30d 14h 27m 2...	
▷ ▶ Checkup Phase										00s	
▷ ▶ Preparation Phase										00s	
▷ ▶ Migration Phase										00s	
▷ ▶ Validation Phase										00s	
▷ ▶ Activation Phase										00s	

Figure 4.10 Example Process Tree for Migration Scenario 3

The next section will describe how to navigate the migration cockpit and show an example of the migration tasks to be performed in the setup phase for migration scenario 3.

Migration Cockpit Navigation and Migration Tasks

The migration cockpit displays the phases as follows:

▶ Setup phase

▶ Checkup phase

▶ Preparation phase

▶ Migration phase

▶ Validation phase

▶ Activation phase

Each phase above contains the tasks you must execute, and you cannot proceed to a new phase until the current phase is complete. In fact, within each phase, in general you cannot proceed with a new task until the previous task has a status of yellow or green.

In the State column the migration cockpit shows which phase is current. In Figure 4.10, you can see that we are presently in the setup phase because there is a truck icon in the State column. The cockpit shows other information such as when the current phase was started (Start Date and Time) and completed (End Date and Time). It also shows the total time that has been spent on the current phase under Run Time.

Figure 4.11 shows an example of the migration tasks for the setup phase.

The general ledger migration cockpit is an excellent tool, and project management should be familiar with it as early as possible in the migration project.

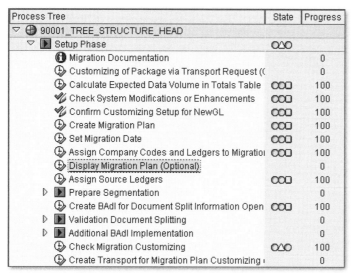

Process Tree	State	Progress
▽ ⊕ 90001_TREE_STRUCTURE_HEAD		
▽ ▶ Setup Phase	○∆○	
ℹ Migration Documentation		0
⊕ Customizing of Package via Transport Request ((		0
⊕ Calculate Expected Data Volume in Totals Table	○○▭	100
✔ Check System Modifications or Enhancements	○○▭	100
✔ Confirm Customizing Setup for NewGL	○○▭	100
⊕ Create Migration Plan	○○▭	100
⊕ Set Migration Date	○○▭	100
⊕ Assign Company Codes and Ledgers to Migratior	○○▭	100
⊕ Display Migration Plan (Optional)		0
⊕ Assign Source Ledgers	○○▭	100
▷ ▶ Prepare Segmentation		0
⊕ Create BAdI for Document Split Information Open	○○▭	100
▷ ▶ Validation Document Splitting		0
▷ ▶ Additional BAdI Implementation		0
⊕ Check Migration Customizing	○∆○	100
⊕ Create Transport for Migration Plan Customizing (		0

Figure 4.11 Migration Tasks in Setup Phase

4.3.4 Migration Project Phases

A migration to SAP General Ledger project can be split into three phases:

▸ Phase 0 — Planning

▸ Phase 1 — Migration and testing

▸ Phase 2 — Go-live

Figure 4.12 shows these three phases of the migration project. Note that the Classic general ledger continues to be used until the date of activation, which is the start of phase 2, the go-live. At this point all documents with a posting date matching or after the date of migration are transferred to the new SAP General Ledger. As stated previously, the date of migration must be a fiscal year change. Because the documents for the prior fiscal year remain in the Classic general ledger, financial statements and other reports can still be generated for the prior fiscal year during phases 1 and 2. This approach guarantees data continuity.

Because the date of migration must be a fiscal year change, it is recommended that you start the planning phase no later than three months before the fiscal year change (and earlier for more complex migrations).

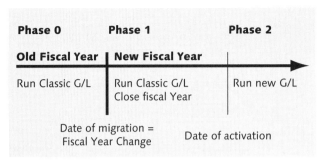

Figure 4.12 Phases of Migration

This section has introduced the five available migration scenarios for migrating from the Classic general ledger. As mentioned previously, many companies that are transitioning to IFRS use either scenario 3 if they do not have an existing parallel reporting solution or scenario 5 if they are switching from using parallel accounts in the Classic general ledger to parallel ledgers in SAP General Ledger. In both of these cases, after the migration they are able to use the parallel ledgers, segment reporting, document splitting, and foreign currency valuation functionality described in Chapter 3.

The next section explains three new migration scenarios that can be used by companies that are already using SAP General Ledger but that want to add new functionality such as document splitting or parallel ledgers for their transition to IFRS.

4.4 SAP General Ledger Migration Scenarios for IFRS

Originally, there were only five migration scenarios, all of which were for migrating from the Classic general ledger to SAP General Ledger. SAP then introduced three new scenarios as follows for the subsequent implementation of new functionality when already using SAP General Ledger:

▶ Scenario 6: Subsequent implementation of document splitting
▶ Scenario 7: Subsequent implementation of a parallel ledger

▶ Scenario 8: Subsequent change from a parallel accounts solution to a parallel ledgers solution

Many companies are using these new migration scenarios as part of their transition to IFRS because, for example, during their original implementation, document splitting and parallel ledgers may not have been required but are now owing to IFRS requirements.

Two prerequisites for using the new migration scenarios are:

▶ SAP General Ledger must be live

▶ The SAP migration service must be used

> **Note**
>
> Several of CAPE Global Consulting's customers have wanted to implement both document splitting and parallel ledgers. However, it is important to note that these new migration scenarios cannot be performed at the same time. For example, if a customer requires scenarios 6 and 7, they must perform a migration project for scenario 6 at the end of one fiscal year and then another migration project for scenario 7 at the end of the following fiscal year.

This section will explain the three new migration scenarios with more focus on migration scenarios 7 and 8 because many companies will be required to add a parallel ledger for their transition to IFRS. For example, many of the scenarios discussed in Section 3.2 for companies already using SAP systems require the use of scenarios 7 and 8.

The process for initiating a migration using one of these new migration scenarios (6-8) is similar to migration scenarios 1-5, and one of the first things to do is to complete an SAP questionnaire.

4.4.1 SAP Questionnaire for Migration Scenarios 6-8

As mentioned previously, there is a different SAP questionnaire for scenarios 6-8 than for scenarios 1-5. Both questionnaires can be downloaded from *http://service.sap.com/GLMIG*. A sample of the questions for parallel reporting in the questionnaire for migration scenarios 6-8 is as follows:

Parallel reporting	
Do you use parallel accounting within new G/L?	Yes/No
Do you intend to implement parallel accounting in the new G/L?	Yes/No
Current approach for parallel accounting within new G/L:	
Account approach	Yes/No
Ledger approach	Yes/No
Future approach for parallel accounting within new G/L:	
Account approach	Yes/No
Ledger approach	Yes/No
Which is your accounting principle in the new G/L leading ledger?	
IFRS	Yes/No
US-GAAP	Yes/No
Local Legislation	Yes/No
Another type	Yes/No
Which accounting principle do you currently use in depreciation area 01 in asset accounting (FI-AA)?	
IFRS	Yes/No
US-GAAP	Yes/No
Local Legislation	Yes/No
Another type	Yes/No

The answers to these questions enable SAP to determine whether you require scenario 7 or scenario 8. For example, if a company uses the parallel accounts solution today but wants to uses parallel ledgers in the future, they will require scenario 8. The question about depreciation area 01 is important because depreciation area 01 must be the same accounting principle as the leading ledger.

A sample of the questions for document splitting in the questionnaire for migration scenarios 6-8 is as follows:

Configuration of Document Splitting	
Usage of Document Splitting	
Do you already use document splitting in new G/L?	Yes/No
Do you already use document splitting in the SPL?	Yes/No
Activation of document splitting in new G/L	
Do you intend to subsequently implement document splitting?	Yes/No
If you already use document splitting in the new G/L	
We know that changes of the current document splitting customizing are not supported by scenario 6	Yes/No
Company codes where document splitting should be activated:	
Document Splitting Characteristics in New G/L	
Which fields will be defined as document splitting characteristic?	
Business area	Yes/No
Profit center	Yes/No
Segment	Yes/No
Customer field	Yes/No
Another type	Yes/No

As can be seen from the first question for document splitting, you must indicate whether you already use document splitting in SAP General Ledger. This is important because migration scenario 6 is designed to add document splitting configuration, not to change it. If document splitting is used already, migration scenario 6 cannot add new document splitting characteristics or make changes to existing characteristics such as making them mandatory. Migration scenario 6 will be covered in more detail in the next section.

4.4.2   Scenario 6: Subsequent implementation of document splitting

Migration scenario 6 allows companies that are already using SAP General Ledger without document splitting to add document splitting.

Prerequisites

There are several prerequisites for the use of migration scenario 6:

- ► SAP General Ledger must be live.
- ► Document splitting must not be active for any of the company codes being migrated in this scenario.
- ► Company codes to be migrated that have cross-company code postings must be migrated in the same migration plan.
- ► If the document splitting characteristic is to be defined as a mandatory field, for example segment, document summarization must not be active for any of the company codes being migrated in this scenario.
- ► Migration scenario 6 cannot be performed in the same fiscal year as a migration from the Classic general ledger.

Many of the migration tasks and requirements for this scenario are similar to those in migration scenarios 3 and 5, which are also migrations with document splitting but from the Classic general ledger.

Planning Phase Migration Activities

Like all migration scenarios, the migration date for migration scenario 6 must be the first day of a new fiscal year, and similar to migration scenarios 3 and 5, the following activities must take place in the planning phase of the migration project before the migration date:

- ► All document splitting customizing must be tested and transported to the production system but not active.
- ► Validation of document splitting must be activated.
- ► All master data must be set up in the production system, for example, profit centers and segments.

▸ Master data such as profit centers must be assigned to other data such as materials, and segments must be assigned to profit centers.

▸ The correct scenarios must be assigned to the leading ledger. For example, to use document splitting with segments, the profit center update and segmentation scenarios must be assigned to the leading ledger.

▸ Interfaces must be reviewed and modified to accommodate the document splitting characteristic. For example, if segment is to be mandatory for document splitting and derived from profit center, all interfaces must post with either profit center or segment.

▸ The migration cockpit must be installed in the production and test system (requires payment for SAP migration service).

The validation of document splitting is a migration cockpit task and can be in the form of the following:

▸ No validation

▸ Validation log

▸ Validation log and warning message (see Figure 4.13)

▸ Error message

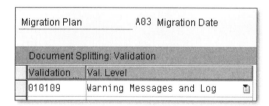

Figure 4.13 Set up Validation of Document Splitting

As soon as validation of document splitting is active, you can generate a validation log using Transaction FAGL_VAL_LOG, which provides a list of all documents posted in production with document splitting errors. This log can also be run directly from the migration cockpit. Figure 4.14 shows an example of the log.

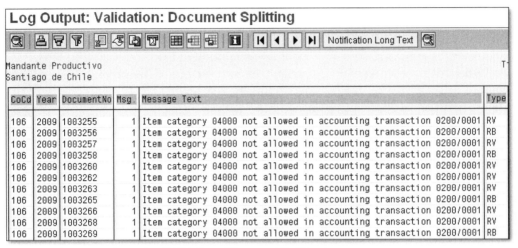

Figure 4.14 Example of Validation of Document Splitting Log

> **Note**
>
> CAPE Global Consulting recommends that customers activate the validation of document splitting as soon as possible before the end of the fiscal year so that any corrections to document splitting customizing can take place before the new fiscal year.

Migration and Testing Phase Migration Activities

This is the phase where multiple test migrations are performed using the migration cockpit. Migrations such as scenario 6 that include document splitting require that you execute two unique migration tasks when building work lists for open items and current year documents as follows:

▶ **Process Document Split for Open Items**

This program adds document splitting information to the open items stored in the previously created open items work list. When the open items were originally posted, document splitting was not active in the system, so the open items must be enriched with the document splitting characteristic. An example of this is if for IFRS purposes you are migrating with document splitting and using segment as your split characteristic. The open items from the previous fiscal year do not contain the Segment field; this must be added during this activity with the BAdI FAGL_MIGR_SUBST.

162

> **Note**
>
> Using a BAdI to enrich the open items is not true document splitting. Only one account assignment can be added per document, so if, for example, you have a vendor open item that should be split between two segments, you must choose one segment for this enrichment process.

Figure 4.15 shows the selection screen for executing this activity. It is strongly recommended that you execute this activity in test mode, with overview + incomplete objects, and always in the background because there can be long runtimes.

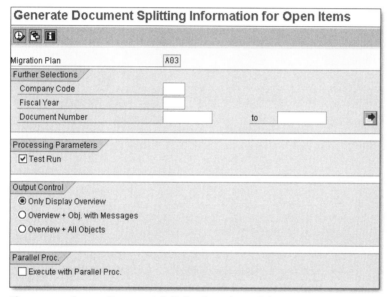

Figure 4.15 Process Document Split for Open Items Selection Screen

All open items processed successfully in this activity have a status of 10 in the table FAGL_MIG_OPITEMS. Open items with errors have a status of 01, and this activity displays the error messages for these items.

▶ **Process Split Information for Documents**
  This activity is also only for migrations with document splitting. It is a different activity from Process Split Information for Open Items because the document splitting customizing was in the system when the current year documents were

posted. With validation of document splitting activated and monitoring of the validation log, most documents should process correctly in this step.

Figure 4.16 shows the selection screen for executing this activity. It is strongly recommended that you execute this activity in test mode, with overview + incomplete objects, and always in the background because there can be long runtimes.

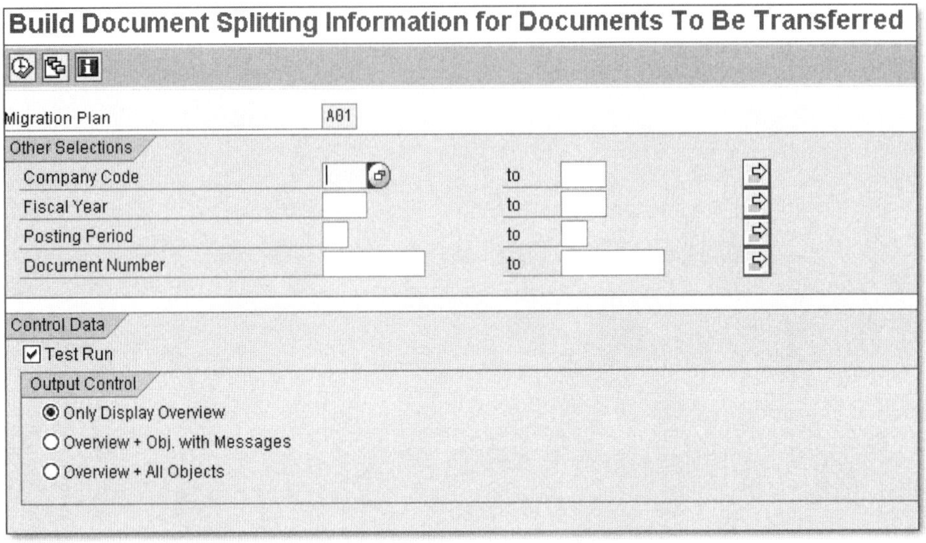

Figure 4.16 Process Split Information for Documents Selection Screen

All documents processed successfully in this activity have a status of 10 in the table FAGL_MIG_RPITEMS. Documents with errors have a status of 01, and this activity displays the error messages for these items.

> **Note**
>
> To add the document splitting characteristic for the balance carry forward of non-open item managed general ledger accounts, you must use the BAdI FAGL_UPLOAD_CF.

When you have completed the SAP questionnaire for scenario 6 and paid for the SAP migration service, SAP provides an access key, and you can install the migration cockpit with the package for scenario 6.

As mentioned previously, many companies now require the document splitting functionality for IFRS because they are required to produce full financial statements by segment. Migration scenario 6 is an excellent solution for this and will help many companies meet the requirements of IFRS 8.

4.4.3 Scenario 7: Subsequent Implementation of an Additional Ledger

Migration scenario 7 allows companies that are already using SAP General Ledger without parallel reporting to add a parallel ledger.

Prerequisites for Scenario 7

There are several prerequisites for the use of migration scenario 7:

- ▶ SAP General Ledger must be live.

- ▶ The additional ledger to be added must be a parallel ledger and cannot be the leading ledger.

- ▶ Any scenarios that are to be assigned to the new ledger must already be assigned to an existing ledger so that the data can be copied. For example, you cannot add the profit center update scenario to the new ledger if the profit center update scenario is not assigned to any existing ledgers.

- ▶ If data will be copied from a parallel ledger to the new ledger, the company codes to be linked to the new ledger must also be linked to the parallel ledger.

- ▶ The new ledger cannot have currencies assigned that are not present in the leading ledger.

- ▶ If document splitting will be required in the new ledger, document splitting must be already active or implemented in a separate migration project using migration scenario 6.

- ▶ Many of the migration tasks and requirements for this scenario are similar to those in migration scenario 4, which is also a migration with parallel ledgers but from the Classic general ledger. Figure 4.17 shows the three phases for migration scenario 7. Note that the new ledger is not actually implemented until the activation date. Similar to other migration scenarios, the main constraint on the activation date is that the previous fiscal year must be closed with no further postings.

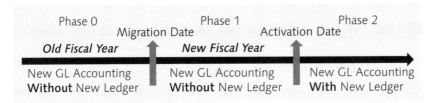

Figure 4.17 Three Phases for Migration Scenario 7

Note

In the period between the migration date and the activation date, postings are made to the new ledger but in the background. However, postings made to the previous fiscal year are not made to the new ledger.

Planning Phase Migration Activities for Scenario 7

Like all migration scenarios, the migration date for this migration scenario must be the first day of a new fiscal year, and similar to migration scenario 4 the following activities must take place in the planning phase of the migration project before the migration date:

▶ The migration cockpit must be installed in the production and test system (requires payment for SAP migration service).

▶ Package 7 for migration scenario 7 must be loaded into the migration cockpit.

▶ The migration plan must be created with assigned company codes.

▶ Customizing including the following must be transported to the production system:

  ▶ Create new parallel ledger.

  ▶ Assign company codes to new ledger.

  ▶ If required, define new accounting principle and assign to new ledger.

  ▶ If required, make changes to FI-AA.

  ▶ If required, make changes to foreign currency valuation for new ledger.

At the end of the planning phase all of the customizing for the new ledger must be in the production system as noted above. This allows ledger-specific postings to be made to the ledger in the migration and testing phase, which will be covered in the next section.

Migration and Testing Phase Activities for Scenario 7

Although the new ledger is not fully implemented until the activation date, you can still make ledger-specific postings to the new ledger in the migration and testing phase (between the migration date and the activation date). However, it is not possible to generate reports from the new ledger until the activation date because the opening balances are not complete until then. Activities to be performed during this phase include:

► Close previous fiscal year.

► Perform test migrations in test system.

► Perform actual migration in production system.

► An overview of the migration cockpit activities to be performed for this scenario is as follows:

  ► Build worklist for open items from previous fiscal year.

  ► Build worklist for current year documents (if customizing for new ledger is in the production system before the migration date, this step is not required).

  ► Create G/L Line Items and Balance Carryforward. This program transfers the open items from the previous year to the SAP General Ledger tables and creates the balance carryforward entries for these open items.

  ► Transfer Balance Carryforward. This program transfers balances for non-open item managed general ledger accounts.

  ► Repost Balance Carryforward manually: Make adjustment postings to balance carryforward if required.

  ► Transfer current year documents — only required if customizing for new ledger was not in production system before the migration date.

  ► Execute FI-AA reconciliation program (RAABST02).

  ► Execute foreign currency valuation for any new valuation areas created for new ledger.

  ► Close migration plan in the migration cockpit.

With migration scenario 7, there are changes to other areas such as new depreciation areas for FI-AA and valuation areas for foreign currency valuation. We will explain these changes in the next sections.

Changes to Asset Accounting for New Ledger in Migration Scenario 7

There are two cases where changes to the asset accounting customizing for the new ledger are required:

1. A new depreciation area is required to post to the new ledger. For example, a U.S. company is using migration scenario 7 to add a new ledger for IFRS and now requires a depreciation area for IFRS.

2. There is an existing depreciation area in asset accounting, but it was not previously set up to post to a ledger. For example, there is a depreciation area for IFRS, but this did not post to the general ledger, and it must now post to the new ledger.

For both cases above, the changes to the asset accounting customizing should occur in the planning phase before the migration date. The customizing required is as follows:

▶ **New depreciation area**

  ▶ Create a new depreciation area and a derived depreciation area.

  ▶ Assign the new ledger to the new depreciation area.

  ▶ Make other changes for the new depreciation area such as the depreciation key.

  ▶ Release the new depreciation area for depreciation postings and the derived depreciation area for APC postings.

  ▶ Build the data for the new depreciation area using the program Automatic Opening of a New Depreciation Area (RAFABNEW).

▶ **Existing depreciation area**

  ▶ Assign the new ledger group to the new depreciation area and change the posting indicator so that the depreciation area updates the general ledger.

Changes to Foreign Currency Valuation for New Ledger in Migration Scenario 7

When a new ledger is added for a new accounting principle such as IFRS, you may require new valuation areas for foreign currency valuation. When you require a new valuation area, the customizing activities are as follows:

▶ Define a new valuation method (or use an existing one).

- ▶ Create a new valuation area.
- ▶ Assign the valuation method to the new valuation area.
- ▶ Assign the accounting principle to the new valuation area.

We explained this customizing in Chapter 3 in the section on foreign currency valuation and translation.

4.4.4 Scenario 8: Switch from Parallel Account to Parallel Ledger

Migration scenario 8 allows companies that are already using SAP General Ledger with the parallel accounts solution to switch to the parallel ledgers solution. An example of when this would be used is a U.S. company that has previously used parallel accounts to enable its Canadian subsidiary to report CA GAAP. It now has to also report by IFRS and requires the added functionality and flexibility that parallel ledgers provide. One of the biggest drawbacks to the parallel accounts solution is the number of general ledger accounts required and the possibility of cross-postings.

The prerequisites for migration scenario 8 are the same as for scenario 7, and the activities for the planning and migration and testing phases are similar to migration scenario 7 as follows.

Planning Phase Migration Activities

- ▶ Migration cockpit must be installed in production system (requires payment for SAP migration service).

- Package 8 for migration scenario 8 must be loaded into the migration cockpit.
- Migration plan must be created with assigned company codes.
- Customizing including the following must be transported to the production system:
  - Create new parallel ledger.
  - Assign company codes to new ledger.
  - If required, define new accounting principle and assign to new ledger.
  - If required, make changes to FI-AA.
  - If required, make changes to foreign currency valuation for new ledger.

At the end of the planning phase all of the customizing for the new ledger must be in the production system as noted above. This allows you to make ledger-specific postings to the ledger in the migration and testing phase, which we will cover in the next section.

Migration and Testing Phase Activities

The general activities to be performed in this phase for migration scenario 8 are similar to scenario 7.

Activities to be performed during this phase include:

- Close previous fiscal year.
- Perform test migrations in test system.
- Perform actual migration in production system.

However, there are additional migration cockpit activities for this scenario. An overview of the migration cockpit activities to be performed for this scenario is as follows:

1. Build worklist for open items from previous fiscal year.

2. Build worklist for current year documents (if customizing for new ledger is in the production system before the migration date, this step is not required).

3. Create G/L Line Items and Balance Carryforward. This program transfers the open items from the previous year to the SAP General Ledger tables and creates the balance carryforward entries for these open items.

4. Transfer Balance Carryforward. This program transfers balances for non-open item managed general ledger accounts. Note that for scenario 8 the parallel accounts that are not relevant for the accounting principle of the new ledger should not be included and should be closed.

  ▶ Repost Balance Carryforward manually. Use Transaction FBCB to manually transfer the balance carryforward from the old parallel accounts to the new ledger.

  ▶ Write off the balance carryforward of the old parallel accounts from the leading ledger.

Figure 4.18 provides an overview of the transfer balance carryforward for scenario 8.

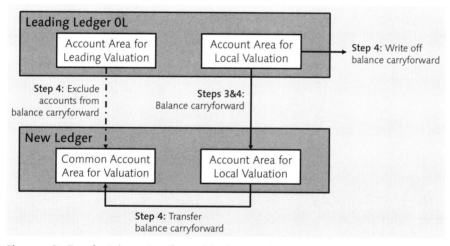

Figure 4.18 Transfer Balance Carryforward for Scenario 8

5. Transfer current year documents. This is only required if customizing for the new ledger was not in the production system before the migration date.

6. Transfer manual postings made to the old parallel accounts to the new ledger common accounts.

7. Transfer current year asset postings made for APC and depreciation from the old parallel accounts to the new ledger common accounts.

8. Execute foreign currency valuation for any new valuation areas created for the new ledger.

Figure 4.19 provides an overview of activities 5-8 above.

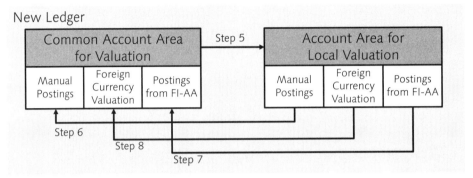

Figure 4.19 Transferring Documents from Phase 1 for Scenario 8

9. Close the migration plan in the migration cockpit.

10. With migration scenario 8, there are changes to other areas such as new depreciation areas for FI-AA and valuation areas for foreign currency valuation. The next sections explain these changes.

Asset Accounting for New Ledger in Migration Scenario 8

The following changes to the asset accounting customizing should occur in the planning phase before the migration:

▶ Assign the new ledger group to the depreciation area that is being converted from posting to parallel accounts to posting parallel ledgers.

▶ Assign the leading ledger group to depreciation area 01 and all other depreciation areas that post to SAP General Ledger.

▶ Create a new derived depreciation area for the depreciation area that is being converted.

> **Note**
>
> The new derived depreciation area must not contain a posting indicator that would cause postings to SAP General Ledger.

At this stage the customizing is set up so that there will be postings to the old parallel accounts in the leading ledger and also to the new ledger common accounts.

You must then perform the following activities for asset accounting during the migration phase:

▶ Execute migration cockpit task Reset Periodic APC Posting Run (RAPERDEL).

▶ Reverse all documents for the periodic APC posted in the current year.

▶ Execute migration cockpit task Store Old Account Determination for FI-AA During Migration (FAGL_COPY_OLD_DETERMINATION).

▶ Change the account determination for the depreciation area to be converted from the old parallel accounts to the new ledger common accounts.

▶ Assign the posting indicator for posting APC to the new derived depreciation area.

▶ Change the posting indicator for the depreciation area to be converted to post depreciation only.

▶ Assign the ledger group for just the new ledger to the depreciation area to be converted and for the new derived depreciation area.

▶ Execute the APC run.

▶ Execute the migration cockpit task Transfer all Depreciation Documents after Migration with New Account Determination (FAGL_MIG_AFA_POST). This program reverses the depreciation documents posted in the current year and transfers them to the new ledger common accounts.

▶ Execute FI-AA reconciliation program (RAABST02).

These activities result in the converted depreciation area posting only to the new ledger common accounts.

Changes to Foreign Currency Valuation for New Ledger in Migration Scenario 8

After the balance carryforward has been completed for the new ledger and all values transferred from the old parallel accounts to the new ledger common accounts, you must perform the following activities for foreign currency valuation:

▶ Reset the foreign currency valuation for the valuation area to be converted. You must do this for every period in the current year.

▶ Change the account assignment for the valuation area to be converted from using the old parallel accounts to the new ledger common accounts.

▶ Assign the new ledger group to the accounting principle of the valuation area to be converted.

▶ Run the foreign currency valuation program for all periods in the current year.

These activities result in foreign currency valuation posting to the new ledger common accounts instead of the old parallel accounts.

4.5   Summary

This chapter has focused on the technical changes to the SAP system that many companies will require for the transition to IFRS. The chapter started with explaining the upgrade process to SAP ERP, which is essential if you want to use the new functionality in SAP General Ledger. Most companies perform a technical upgrade to SAP ERP, which is faster, and new functionality can be added at a later stage.

Section 4.3 then provided an overview of the five migration scenarios that SAP provides for migrations from the Classic general ledger. This section introduced the SAP migration service and provided an overview of the migration cockpit. However, please refer to my other SAP Press book, *Migrate Successfully to the SAP General Ledger,* which provides more detailed information and step-by-step instructions for the migration cockpit tasks. This migration book also contains a case study of one of the largest migrations with document splitting performed by CAPE Global Consulting.

The final section of the chapter described the three new migration scenarios that SAP provides to enable companies to implement functionality such as document splitting and parallel ledgers. These are not really migrations in the true sense because SAP General Ledger must already be in use. Rather, they offer the ability to add the new functionality that is invaluable for IFRS, and the use of the migration cockpit ensures that the tasks required are executed in the correct order.

Many companies implemented SAP General Ledger when IFRS was not part of their thinking, or they did not have enough information to forecast what would be needed for IFRS. Therefore, many companies that did not previously need the document splitting or parallel ledger functionality now require it. Instead of having to perform a reimplementation of their SAP system, they can use the new scenarios to add the new functionality.

The current timeline for IFRS is 2011 for Canada and 2014 for the U.S. (2012 for the start of the dual reporting period). Therefore, there is not much time for companies that need to upgrade and then migrate to SAP General Ledger. Although these technical changes can often be run in parallel with the IFRS accounting project, there is still not much time, and the earlier the technical changes are addressed, the better.

In fact, many Canadian companies that want to use SAP General Ledger for the transition to IFRS in 2011 have little choice now other than to perform a technical upgrade followed immediately by a migration to SAP General Ledger, with a migration date of January 1, 2011, for companies with a calendar fiscal year. The upgrade and migration projects must be separate projects.

The next chapter will explain the various phases in a typical IFRS project. It will explain how the technical changes to SAP systems can be incorporated into the project timeline and describe some of CAPE Global Consulting's IFRS project methodology for assisting with the transition to IFRS.

This chapter introduces the complete project plan for an IFRS transition. The project methodology discussed here is applicable to many IFRS scenarios.

5   IFRS Transition Project

5.1   Introduction

This chapter explains how CAPE Global Consulting assists companies and their accounting teams with their transition to IFRS project. In our experience, the transition requires a methodical approach, and although this chapter will focus on the current U.S. time line, the project methodology is equally applicable to other countries that still have to transition to IFRS such as Brazil and Canada.

5.2   Time Line

Chapter 1 provided details on the countries that still have to transition to IFRS and explained the proposed SEC roadmap for U.S. companies. As a recap for the three main countries discussed in this book, the time lines are as follows:

- **Brazil**
  All listed/public companies and financial institutions will be required to report consolidated financial statements by IFRS starting on January 1, 2010. This has been approved by the Brazilian Securities and Exchange Commission.

- **Canada**
  All listed/public companies must report by IFRS starting on January 1, 2011. This decision was recently confirmed by the AcSB in a bulletin published in May 2009.

▶ **United States**

The current proposal is that U.S. companies will be required to file financial statements by IFRS for fiscal years ending after December 14, 2014. There will be a two-year dual reporting period for U.S. GAAP and IFRS for 2012-2013.

This book has described the accounting standards and key differences between IFRS and the local GAAPs for the three countries listed above. The book has also discussed the changes required in SAP systems for IFRS including the new functionality in SAP General Ledger and upgrading to SAP ERP and how to migrate to SAP General Ledger. Figure 5.1 shows SAP's view of when these accounting and technical changes should take place during the transition to IFRS for a U.S. company.

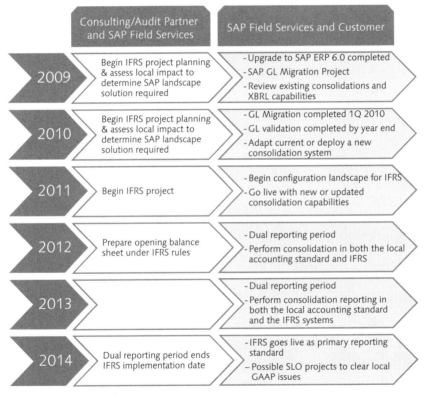

Figure 5.1 Time Line for IFRS Activities

SAP recommends that the technical changes such as an upgrade or migration run in parallel with the IFRS accounting project. For Brazil and Canada, there is no choice because the deadlines are so close, and therefore the upgrade and migration projects must start immediately with the IFRS accounting project running in parallel. For example, if a Canadian company still has to upgrade and migrate, it is likely that the upgrade project will be early in 2010, and the migration date will most likely be January 1, 2011, if the company is on a calendar fiscal year. At the same time, the Canadian company must be running its IFRS accounting project in parallel.

The first step in an IFRS project is to evaluate the impact of IFRS on your company. The next section will discuss this and other phases in the project.

5.3   Project Phases

CAPE Global Consulting has four phases in a typical transition to IFRS project. The first phase is to review the impact of IFRS on the organization both financially and from a systems standpoint. The second phase is to define the project plan, having identified the requirements, and the third and fourth phases are the realization and go-live, respectively. Figure 5.2 shows an overview of the four phases and some of the activities performed.

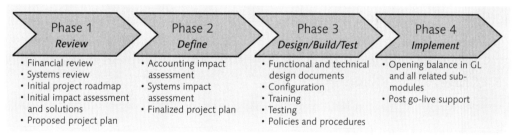

Figure 5.2 Phases of an IFRS Project

The next section provides a more detailed explanation of the activities to be performed.

5.3.1   Phase 1: Review

The key activities in this phase are as follows.

Financial Review

Assess the items in the financial statements that will be impacted by IFRS. Examples include revenue recognition, inventory, leases, and so on. The accounting department performs this activity, and the accounting impacts will determine the SAP components that will be impacted. Figure 5.3 shows an example of the CAPE Global Consulting matrix for highlighting the SAP components impacted by IFRS.

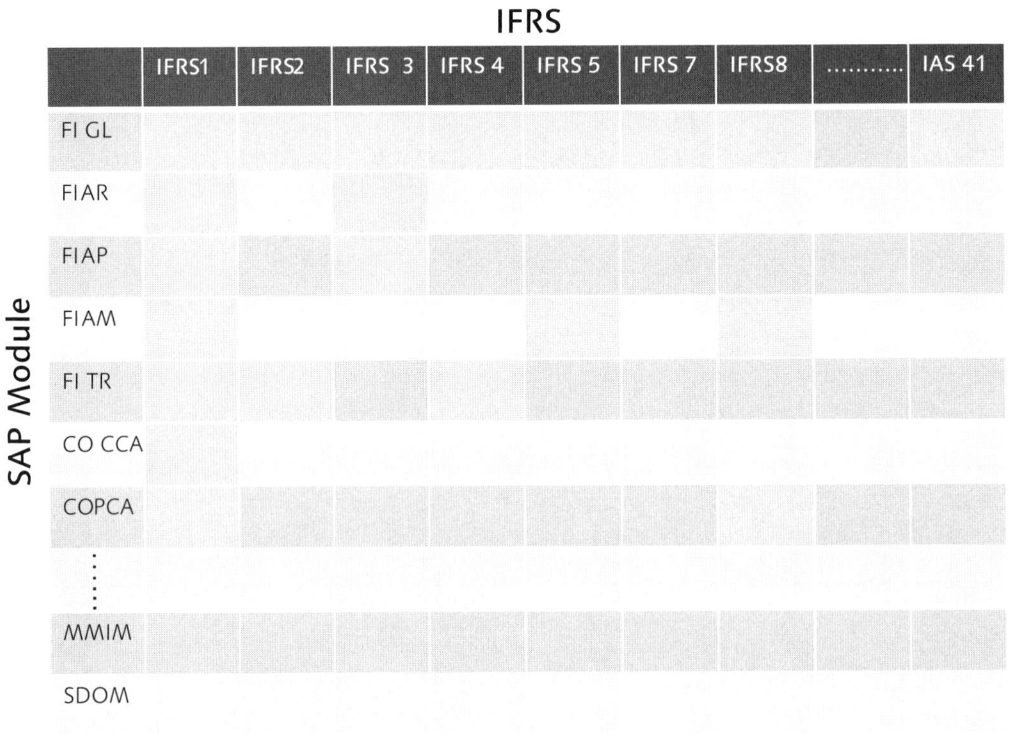

IFRS

SAP Module	IFRS1	IFRS2	IFRS 3	IFRS 4	IFRS 5	IFRS 7	IFRS8	....	IAS 41
FI GL									
FI AR									
FI AP									
FI AM									
FI TR									
CO CCA									
COPCA									
MMIM									
SDOM									

Figure 5.3 Example of Matrix Showing Impact of IFRS on SAP Components

Systems Review

The first decision to make in the systems review is to determine whether an upgrade to SAP ERP and a migration to SAP General Ledger are required. We have already covered this in detail, but there may be other system changes that are required such as SLO services to change asset depreciation areas, convert chart of accounts, and so on. Also, the method of consolidation and ability to generate XBRL must be reviewed. The transition to IFRS is an excellent opportunity to improve SAP systems, and CAPE Global Consulting can assist with all tasks such as clean-up of master data, reconfiguration of SAP components, and so on. Also included in the systems review is the impact of IFRS on legacy systems.

Initial Project Roadmap

Figure 5.1 shows some of the typical accounting and technical changes that will be required for a U.S. company. Having assessed the financial and system impacts, CAPE then delivers an initial project roadmap showing when the changes specific to the company need to be made. There are many different initial situations that impact the roadmap; for example, some companies have already upgraded to SAP ERP but have not migrated to SAP General Ledger. Other companies have upgraded and migrated but require one of the new migration scenarios 6-8 to implement new functionality, and these all impact the roadmap.

Initial Impact Assessment and Solutions

This document details all of the financial and system impacts of IFRS and proposes solutions. An example is IAS 16, which requires components of assets to be depreciated. If this will impact the company, the solution is usually to make changes to the asset master data.

Proposed Project Plan

This document details how the IFRS project should be structured such as the steering committee, project management, accounting resources, consultants, and so on. CAPE Global Consulting has found that a full-time project manager, for example, is essential for the transition to IFRS.

> **Note**
>
> It is extremely important that a company such as CAPE Global Consulting review the SAP system setup for the IFRS project as early as possible in this first phase. Many of the solutions proposed for the financial impacts such as IFRS 8, Operating Segments, may depend on SAP functionality in SAP General Ledger that must be in place as soon as possible.

5.3.2 Phase 2: Define

The key activities in this phase are the following.

Accounting Impact Assessment

A financial review is conducted in phase 1, but this is the final assessment of the impact of IFRS on the financial statements. This document describes the accounting differences between the current local GAAP (such as U.S. GAAP) and IFRS. It proposes solutions for the differences, for example, using segment reporting in SAP General Ledger for IFRS 8. There may also be other gaps such as to how to produce financial statements by IFRS before SAP General Ledger is active. One solution for this is to use parallel accounts in the Classic general ledger. This document also quantifies the effect of the IFRS accounting changes on significant financial statement items such as goodwill, profit, taxes, and so on.

Systems Impact Assessment

A systems review is conducted in phase 1, but this is the final assessment of the IT changes that must be made for the transition to IFRS. This document contains a roadmap detailing when to make the IT changes and includes resource requirements such as budget and staffing. Many initial situations impact the IT assessment. For example, companies may have multiple SAP production systems, possibly with different SAP system releases.

Finalized Project Plan

Finally, in this phase a detailed project plan is created containing all planning for the project. This includes timing, staffing, scope, and so on and must be approved by the project management and steering committee before phase 3 can be started.

5.3.3 Phase 3: Design/Build/Test

The key activities in this phase are as follows.

Functional and Technical Design Documents

Documentation is created for all functional and technical changes that will be made in the SAP system for the transition to IFRS.

Configuration

Changes are made in the system for IFRS. These include, for example, the use of segments to meet IFRS 8 requirements, changing asset master data to meet the IAS 16 requirements, and so on.

Training

Training is a very important part of the transition to IFRS. End users must be trained in the SAP General Ledger functionality such as parallel ledgers, document splitting, and segments, but IFRS may also impact the following areas that users must be trained on:

▶ **Financial reporting**
  IFRS will require new reports, and some of these may need to be developed.

▶ **Changes to other SAP components**
  In addition to the need for SAP General Ledger training, other components such as materials and asset management will be impacted by IFRS.

▶ **Changes to chart of accounts**
  New accounts may be required for IFRS, or perhaps a change has been made from parallel accounts to parallel ledgers.

▶ **Consolidation**
  Training will be required for consolidation for IFRS and the use of XBRL.

Testing

All IFRS-related changes must be tested before phase 4. For U.S. companies testing must be complete before IFRS is required for the dual reporting period 2012-2013.

Policies and Procedures

There will be many new policies and procedures relating to IFRS, for example, how to manage IFRS and local GAAPs using parallel ledgers in SAP General Ledger. There will also be many new procedures that need to be implemented and documented relating to the different accounting rules.

5.3.4   Phase 4: Go-Live

The key activities in this phase are:

- **Opening balance in SAP General Ledger and all related sub-components**
  Before the start of the new fiscal year, the company's internal accountants and external auditors must verify the opening balances for IFRS.

- **Post go-live support**
  CAPE Global Consulting offers post go-live support for month end, quarter end, and year end close. We also assist with training and any technical problems relating to new functionality such as parallel ledgers, document splitting, segment reporting, and foreign currency valuation.

5.4   What Should You Be Doing Now?

For many companies in countries such as Canada that have to transition to IFRS in 2011, the planning described in phases 1 and 2 in Section 5.3 should have started. In our experience, the transition to IFRS including system changes takes 2-3 years as an upgrade to SAP ERP followed by a migration to the SAP General Ledger, which alone usually takes 12-18 months.

Therefore, U.S. companies that at present have a deadline of 2012 for dual reporting should be starting phase 1 immediately and planning their system changes for IFRS. The SAP system changes should be started as soon as possible, and these are:

- Upgrade to SAP ERP 6.0
- Migrate to the new SAP General Ledger

As mentioned previously, many U.S. companies have not started their transition to IFRS project, but the more time that is spent during phase 1 assessing the current systems and the financial and organizational impacts, the more successful the project will be.

IFRS is definitely coming to the U.S., and U.S. companies need to assess the impact of the IFRS transition project now while there is time to develop the optimal solution. As mentioned in the previous section, the IFRS transition project provides an excellent opportunity to improve systems and procedures. For example, replacing an existing consolidation system with the SAP BusinessObjects Planning and Consolidation (BPC) component will provide many benefits.

5.5 Success Factors

CAPE Global Consulting has been the consulting partner for several IFRS transition projects using SAP ERP Financials, and we have identified several key success factors:

1. **Consulting partner's SAP expertise**
   The consulting partner must have consultants that are experts in the SAP components that are most impacted by IFRS such as SAP General Ledger, Asset Management, Materials Management, Consolidation, and so on.

2. **Consulting partner's accounting expertise**
   The consulting partner must understand the IFRS accounting requirements to customize the SAP system. The partner must be able to translate the requirements from the internal accountants and external auditors to provide the optimal SAP solution.

3. **Identify in phase 1 the financial impact of differences between IFRS and the local GAAP**
   The earlier the accounting differences are identified, the more time will be available to either change current accounting procedures or, when that is not possible, to implement new SAP functionality such as segment reporting.

4. **Training**
   Do not underestimate training. As explained in Section 5.3.3, training is a significant part of the project. An IFRS project impacts most of the organization because there are both accounting and system changes.

5.6 Summary

This chapter has explained some of the activities that CAPE Global Consulting recommends for each phase of an IFRS transition project. The chapter started with a recap of the IFRS timelines for the countries still to transition to IFRS such as Brazil, Canada, and the U.S. Figure 5.1 showed the SAP-recommended activities for a U.S. company transitioning to IFRS, and it should be noted that activities such as the upgrade to SAP ERP 6.0 start in 2009. This means SAP is recommending that by the time this book is published, the IFRS project for a U.S. company should already have started.

This is based on the current SEC roadmap, but it demonstrates again that the transition to IFRS is a significant project, and it will usually take two to three years to perform all activities and to begin reporting by IFRS.

One of the first activities during the review phase 1 is to perform a systems review. If an upgrade to SAP ERP 6.0 and a migration to SAP General Ledger are required, these two projects alone will require 12-18 months, and it is very important to understand the required systems changes as early as possible. There may also be changes to legacy systems and to the current consolidation application. Another important point to note is that systems and IT costs are a major component of the total budget for the IFRS transition.

This book should help you start to plan your transition to IFRS using SAP ERP Financials and put you in a position to utilize the many benefits of SAP General Ledger. As mentioned previously in this chapter, strong project management is required for an IFRS transition project, and you also need accounting and technical expertise.

IFRS is coming to the U.S. very soon, and it is a complex transition project requiring significant effort and expertise. We hope this book has conveyed this message and has helped explain some of the functionality within SAP ERP Financials that you can use to meet the IFRS requirements.

The final chapter is a case study and details one of the first transitions to IFRS in Latin America. CAPE Global Consulting assisted with this IFRS project preparing the SAP system, and the chapter will describe the various phases of the project, the key lessons learned, and how typical IFRS problems were overcome.

6   Case Study

This chapter will detail a recent transition to IFRS by a large multinational company, CMPC, which is headquartered in Santiago, Chile. This IFRS project covered most of the topics in this book including an upgrade to SAP ERP and a migration to SAP General Ledger. All of the new SAP functionality recommended for IFRS such as parallel ledgers, document splitting, segment reporting, and foreign currency valuation and translation was implemented during this project and assisted by CAPE Global Consulting. This was one of the first transitions to IFRS in Latin America

The aim of this chapter is to describe the transition to IFRS project for CMPC and to outline the key findings.

6.1   Introduction

In 2006, in its Office Circular No. 368, the Chilean Securities and Insurance Supervisor (SVS) stated that listed companies must report by IFRS from January 1, 2009, with comparative figures for 2008. Subsequently, in the Office Circular No. 427 of 2007, the SVS provided further criteria for the transition to IFRS, and only large companies were required to meet the January 1, 2009, deadline. Other companies, depending on their size, would have to transition to IFRS on either January 1, 2010, or January 1, 2011.

CMPC is one of the largest companies in Chile, and they started their transition to IFRS in August 2007. As part of the system review in phase 1 they decided to upgrade to SAP ERP and migrate to SAP General Ledger. The upgrade was planned for late 2007, with the migration planning starting in March 2008 and a migration date of January 1, 2009.

In March 2008, the CMPC project manager for the IFRS project, Eduardo Jure, contacted CAPE Global Consulting for assistance with the IFRS project and specifically the SAP General Ledger functionality.

6.2 CMPC

CMPC has 45 SAP company codes in three countries: Chile, Argentina, and Peru. CMPC also has companies in Brazil, Uruguay, Mexico, and Ecuador, but these do not use SAP systems.

CMPC has several business divisions including forestry and wood products, pulp, tissue products, paper and paper converted products, and so on.

CMPC has over 2,000 SAP users. All SAP company codes have Financial Accounting and Controlling (CO) implemented, and the main company in Chile uses the SAP components materials management, material ledger, sales and distribution, production planning, plant maintenance, quality management, project system, human resources, and business intelligence.

As part of their IFRS project, CMPC decided that it must migrate to SAP General Ledger to use parallel ledgers, segment reporting with document splitting, and real time integration with CO.

6.3 IFRS Project Phases

CMPC started its transition to IFRS in August 2007 and reported financial statements by IFRS for the first time for the quarter ending March 31, 2009. This was a very efficient project, because most large companies require two to three years for the transition to IFRS.

This section will explain the activities that CMPC performed, with examples of the corresponding documentation in each of the four phases of the IFRS project.

6.3.1 Phases 1 and 2: Review and Define

Owing to time constraints, phases 1 and 2 were combined and took place between August 2007 and January 2008. Some of the activities were as follows:

Financial review

This is one of the first tasks in the project, and CMPC identified the following SAP components and financial statement items that would be most impacted by IFRS. CMPC also identified some of the key tasks for each area:

- **Financial accounting**
  - Ability to report by three accounting principles (IFRS, local GAAP, and tax)
  - Change functional currency to U.S. dollars for company codes other than the tissue division
  - Ability to feed management reports with IFRS principles
  - Modify all accounting interfaces from external systems (over 130 interfaces)
  - Ability to report by operating segments

- **Materials management (inventory)**
  - Materials purchased must include purchase costs and indirect costs for IFRS.
  - Materials produced must include direct costs and indirect costs.
  - Restatements required for local GAAP and tax reporting.

- **Asset management – (fixed assets)**
  - Parallel reporting for assets for IFRS, local GAAP, and tax
  - How to manage impairments
  - Ability to report by asset components
  - How to manage future revaluations
  - How to generate comparative reporting for 2008
  - How to account for business combinations

- **Revenue recognition and tax**
  - How to recognize revenue only when risk transferred to customer

- ▶ Taxes on export sales

- ▶ Deferred taxes

▶ **Financial instruments: derivatives**

    ▶ How to value derivatives such as forwards, swaps at mark to market

This was the initial financial review, and these were the areas that CMPC believed would be most impacted by the transition to IFRS.

> **Note**
>
> At this stage, CMPC only considered companies which used SAP.

Systems Review

At the start of the IFRS project in 2007, CMPC was using SAP R/3, and it was decided that CMPC must upgrade to SAP ERP and then migrate to SAP General Ledger. At that time no other companies in Latin America had migrated to SAP General Ledger, and the project manager was given the task of finding more information and a suitable consulting company.

In addition to the upgrade and migration, CMPC also reviewed its many interfaces with external systems and considered whether they would be required with SAP General Ledger and if so, how they would be modified.

Finally, in this initial systems review, CMPC considered its method of producing consolidated financial statements and XBRL. The thinking at this stage was to retain the Strategic Enterprise Management – Business Consolidation System application to consolidate both SAP and non-SAP systems and use a separate SAP application for XBRL. Figure 6.1 shows an overview of the proposed consolidation.

Initial Project Roadmap

The roadmap for CMPC showed the activities that would be performed in each of the four phases of the project. CMPC planned to upgrade to SAP ERP 6.0 as soon as possible and in parallel to the other accounting activities. Phase 3 during 2008 would thus include preparation for a migration to SAP General Ledger and testing in a pilot system of the new functionality such as parallel ledgers, document splitting, and segment reporting. Figure 6.2 shows the roadmap and the timing of the CMPC transition to IFRS.

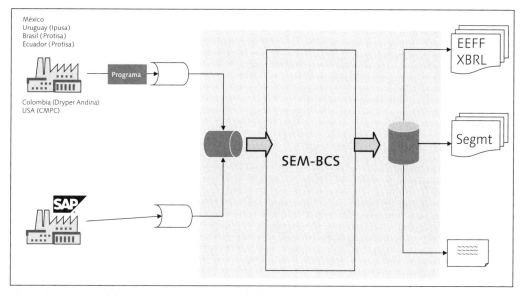

Figure 6.1 Proposed Structure for Financial Consolidation

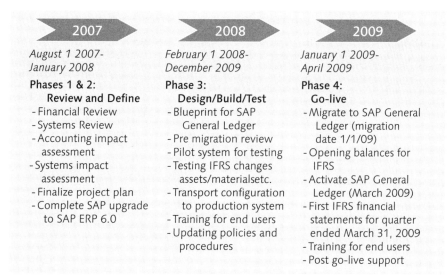

2007	2008	2009
August 1 2007- *January 2008*	*February 1 2008-* *December 2009*	*January 1 2009-* *April 2009*

Phases 1 & 2:
Review and Define
- Financial Review
- Systems Review
- Accounting impact
  assessment
- Systems impact
  assessment
- Finalize project plan
- Complete SAP upgrade
  to SAP ERP 6.0
	Phase 3:
	Design/Build/Test
	- Blueprint for SAP
	  General Ledger
	- Pre migration review
	- Pilot system for testing
	- Testing IFRS changes
	  assets/materialsetc.
	- Transport configuration
	  to production system
	- Training for end users
	- Updating policies and
	  procedures
		Phase 4:
		Go-live
		- Migrate to SAP General
		  Ledger (migration
		  date 1/1/09)
		- Opening balances for
		  IFRS
		- Activate SAP General
		  Ledger (March 2009)
		- First IFRS financial
		  statements for quarter
		  ended March 31, 2009
		- Training for end users
		- Post go-live support

Figure 6.2 Initial Roadmap for CMPC IFRS Project

Initial Impact Assessment and Solutions

Having completed the financial and systems review, CMPC then created a document detailing the proposed solutions. Table 6.1 shows some of the impacts of the IFRS project and the proposed solutions.

IFRS Impact/Requirement	Proposed Solution
Maintain three accounting principles: IFRS, local GAAP, and tax	Migrate to SAP General Ledger and implement parallel ledgers functionality
Report by operating segment as per IFRS 8	Migrate to SAP General Ledger and implement segment reporting with document splitting functionality
Include indirect costs as part of product cost	For domestic products create condition types for indirect costs to be added to purchase orders when appropriate For imports, must implement new model
Consider all manufacturing overhead costs as part of the cost of production (absorption) without affecting the internal management of current costs (direct)	Implement a "distribution" in the CO component and do not modify the current bills of material The result of the distribution will be posted to inventory and cost of sales manually and only to the IFRS (leading) ledger
Revenue recognition: Do not recognize revenue for IFRS until risks and rewards are transferred to customer	Do not make changes to the accounting of actual sales. Incorporate incoterms in the header of each sales invoice voucher; this voucher may have been generated from the SAP system or from a legacy system interface Develop a program running on a monthly basis and identify sales incoterms DDU and DDP during the month Reverse the identified sales for IFRS only (income and cost of sales) and immediately cancel this effect on first of the following month

Table 6.1 CMPC Initial Impact Assessment and Solutions

IFRS Impact/Requirement	Proposed Solution
Measure biological assets at fair value less estimated point of sale costs as per IAS 41	Determine the replacement cost of each material. Save the replacement cost in the material master for further calculations and reports, without replacing the current price for the valuation of the movements
Export sales should not include excise tax, surcharges, and discounts	Use the CO-PA (profitability analysis) component to determine the amount of export sales for the month
	Make a posting for IFRS only using Transaction FB50L with the values in this report
Identification of the RLI and deferred taxes	Use fixed assets module to post valuation to tax parallel ledger
	Use accounting transactions such as FB50L in SAP General Ledger that allow you to post specific tax entries to the tax ledger
	Use standard reports in SAP General Ledger to generate reports for only the tax parallel ledger
Value derivatives such as forwards, swaps at mark to market	Today there is a solution developed in Access (Tradex) that performs the monthly calculation to mark to market and integrates with SAP. Continue to use this solution and adapt for SAP General Ledger
	With respect to swaps, continue to also use the existing solution for valuation
For fixed assets, require different depreciation for IFRS, local GAAP, and tax	Set up new depreciation areas (see Table 6.2) and link to new parallel ledgers in SAP General Ledger
Manage impairments, business combinations, and revaluations	
Many of the postings from forestry systems via interfaces will only be valid for the current accounting principles and not IFRS	All interfaces will need to be reviewed and modified to post to relevant ledgers in SAP General Ledger

Table 6.1 CMPC Initial Impact Assessment and Solutions (Cont.)

Depreciation Area	Description	Real/ Derived	Post to G/L	Ledger
01	IFRS	Real	1	OL
02	Tax	Real	3	L2
03	Local GAAP	Real	3	L1
04	Consolidated without revaluation	Real	0	
05	Local GAAP group currency	Real	0	
06	IFRS group currency	Real	0	
07	Tax group currency	Real	0	
20	Revaluation IFRS local currency	Real	0	
21	Revaluation IFRS group currency	Real	0	
22	Business combination local currency	Real	0	
23	Business combination group currency	Real	0	
24	Impairment local currency	Real	0	
25	Impairment group currency	Real	0	
50	Delta 02-01	Derived	6	L2
51	Delta 03-01	Derived	6	L1
52	Delta 05-06	Derived	0	
53	Delta 07-06	Derived	0	

Table 6.2 CMPC Proposed Asset Depreciation Areas

Proposed Project Plan

A significant part of the initial project plan was to determine the project structure. Figure 6.3 shows the proposed project structure for the CMPC transition to IFRS project.

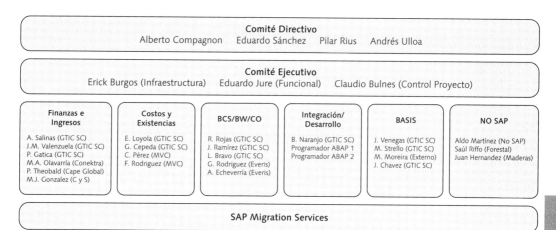

Figure 6.3 CMPC Project Structure for IFRS Project

Accounting Impact Assessment

Having previously determined the areas that would be impacted by IFRS and proposed initial solutions, CMPC then estimated the financial impact for these areas. Some examples are shown in Table 6.3. (amounts shown are examples and not the actual amounts).

Area Impacted	Existing Valuation	IFRS Valuation	Financial Impact
Fixed assets	Purchase cost adjusted for inflation less depreciation	Either purchase cost less depreciation or fair value less depreciation	The application of fair value would generate an increase in fixed assets of $4,000,000 and an increase in depreciation expense of $500,000
Biological assets	Forest plantations are valued at economic value	Valued at fair value	Increase in revaluation reserve of $3,000,000
Product costing	Inventory valued at direct cost	Inventory valued at direct cost plus indirect costs	Increase in inventory of $1,000,000

Table 6.3 Examples of the Financial Impact of IFRS

Area Impacted	Existing Valuation	IFRS Valuation	Financial Impact
Revenue recognition	Some export sales recognized as income immediately	Export sales must only be recognized as income when risks and rewards passed to customer	Estimated that $5,000,000 of sales income will be deferred under IFRS

Table 6.3 Examples of the Financial Impact of IFRS (Cont.)

These estimated accounting impacts were also shown in consolidated financial statements. Figure 6.4 shows an extract from the consolidated balance sheet with example figures.

Consolidated Balance Sheet
On December 31, 2007

	IFRS USD	ACTUAL USD	DIFFERENCE USD
Assets			
Current Assets			
Accounts Receivable	5,000,000	5,000,000	
Inventory	7,000,000	6,000,000	1,000,000
Other current assets	2,000,000	2,000,000	
Total Current Assets	**14,000,000**	**13,000,000**	**1,000,000**
Biological Assets (Forestry)	**20,000,000**	**17,000,000**	**3,000,000**
Fixed Assets	**25,000,000**	**21,000,000**	**4,000,000**
Other Assets			
Investments in related companies	2,000,000	1,500,000	500,000
Total Other Assets	**2,000,000**	**1,500,000**	**500,000**
Total Assets	**61,000,000**	**52,500,000**	**8,500,000**

Figure 6.4 Example of IFRS Accounting Impact on Financial Statements

Systems Impact Assessment

The main systems impact for CMPC was the upgrade to SAP ERP and then the migration to SAP General Ledger. The upgrade was started in late 2007, with the migration planning scheduled to start in March 2008. The systems impact assessment included a budget for these changes and assessed the impact of SAP General Ledger on interfaces and reports. Legacy systems were also reviewed to understand how they would be impacted.

Finalized Project Plan

Finally, a full project plan incorporating all of the information for the project was finalized and approved by the executive committee.

6.3.2   Phase 3: Design/Build/Test

Phase 3 of the transition to IFRS project for CMPC started in February 2008. This is the phase where the main activities were the configuration of the IFRS changes, the testing of the changes, and the training of end users. These and other activities performed during this phase were as follows:

Functional and Technical Design Documents

In March 2008, CAPE Global Consulting performed a premigration review service for CMPC. This service explained the new functionality in SAP General Ledger and how a migration project should be run and included a review of the current production system. In the final report CAPE documented how SAP General Ledger should be configured for CMPC (see extract in Figure 6.5) and the time line for the migration project (see Figure 6.6) and recommended data that should be cleaned up in the production system before the migration.

7.6.3 Segments

CMPC will create six segments. As CMPC will use segment as its document splitting characteristic, the IMG tasks should be completed in the planning phase. The relevant IMG tasks are:

> **Define Segment** - Create the six segments:
> - Forestry
> - Pulp
> - Paper
> - Tissue
> - Converted Products
> - Others

Note: CMPC will also have to maintain the segment field on all profit center master records. This should be done using the mass maintenance function.

Figure 6.5   Extract from Premigration Review Report

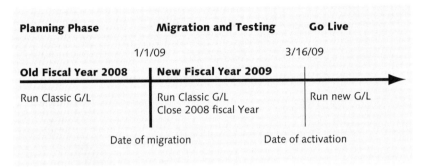

Figure 6.6 Time Line for CMPC Migration Project

The premigration review report was very detailed and contained the functional design required for SAP General Ledger to meet many of the IFRS requirements. Other functional and technical design documentation for IFRS changes such as changes to interfaces was also produced during this phase.

Configuration

In this activity all of the configuration for IFRS had to be completed. Many of the configuration changes were related to SAP General Ledger such as document splitting, segments, parallel ledgers, and so on, but there were also many changes to product costing and asset accounting for CMPC.

A summary of how SAP General Ledger was set up for CMPC and their IFRS requirements is as follows:

► Six segments created
  ► Forestry
  ► Pulp
  ► Paper
  ► Tissue
  ► Converted products
  ► Services and investments
► Leading ledger 0L for IFRS and two parallel ledgers
  ► L1 – Chile local GAAP

- ► L2 – Tax
- ▶ Document splitting by segment and active for all company codes

Training

In June 2008 CAPE Global Consulting conducted training sessions for the CMPC IFRS project team and some end users. The training covered the SAP General Ledger functionality and how the data in the Classic general ledger would be migrated. Personnel from the CMPC finance and IT departments also provided training on IFRS and the impacts on CMPC.

Testing

The premigration review report recommended that CMPC should have a pilot system during 2008 with SAP General Ledger active. In June 2008 CAPE Global Consulting set up the pilot system. This allowed the CMPC IFRS team to become familiar with the new functionality, and several changes were made to the original design. It also allowed testing of the IFRS changes to product costing and asset accounting and existing interfaces and reports. The pilot was just a copy of an existing development client (in a different development system), and the new SAP General Ledger was activated without migration. The SAP General Ledger configuration such as document splitting, segments, parallel ledgers, and real-time integration with CO was then set up.

As an example of the testing performed in the pilot system, CMPC was going to use the segment reporting functionality to meet the IFRS 8 requirement, and as noted above six segments were created. During the testing these segments were linked to profit center master records. Figures 6.7 and 6.8 show two examples. As can be seen in Figure 6.7, profit center 104100 has been linked to segment 3000, which is the paper operating segment.

In Figure 6.8 profit center 104563 has been linked to segment 2000, which is the pulp operating segment.

An accounts payable document was then posted using both of these profit centers as shown in Figure 6.9. One line item is posted to the vendor for 11,900 CLP, and the offset postings are to expense accounts and tax.

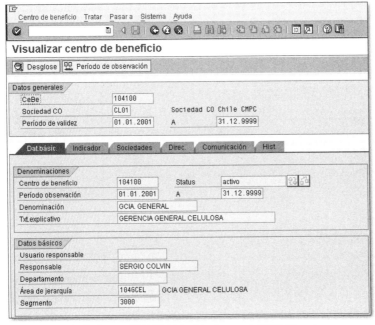

Figure 6.7 Profit Center 104100 Linked to Segment 3000 (Paper)

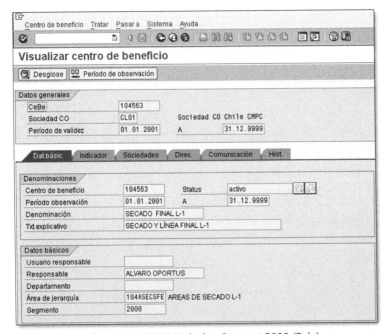

Figure 6.8 Profit Center 104563 Linked to Segment 2000 (Pulp)

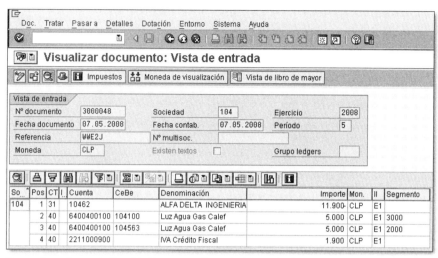

Figure 6.9 Accounts Payable Document Posted with Multiple Segments

Figure 6.10 shows the effect of document splitting with segment on this document (the general ledger view). As can be seen, the accounts payable account (2151000100) and tax account (2211000900) have been split by segment in the same proportion as the expense account.

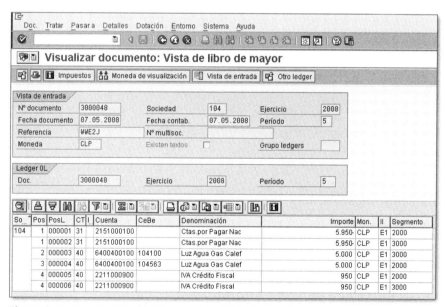

Figure 6.10 Accounts Payable Document 'Split' by Segment

The result of this posting is that CMPC can produce fully balanced financial statements by operating segment.

As part of the testing, CMPC also performed test migrations in a separate quality assurance system. The production system was copied into the new quality assurance system, and three test migrations were performed in October 2008 and January and February 2009. This helped ensure a successful migration in the production system on March 14, 2009.

Policies and procedures

During this phase CMPC updated its policies and procedures relating to the new accounting rules and the system changes.

6.3.3 Phase 4: Go-Live

The migration date for CMPC was January 1, 2009, but the activation date for SAP General Ledger was not until March 15, 2009. Therefore, the target date for reporting by IFRS for the first time was the quarter that ended March 31, 2009. After a successful migration on March 15, 2009, CMPC had the new functionality such as parallel ledgers, document splitting, and segment reporting available for 2009. Some of the remaining activities during this go-live phase were as follows:

▶ **Opening balance in general ledger and all related subcomponents**
CMPC had to make adjustment entries to the opening balances for the IFRS differences. The CMPC internal accountants and external auditors verified these. Because CMPC now had the parallel ledger functionality, adjustments were also made to parallel ledgers L1 and L2 for Chile local GAAP and tax, respectively.

▶ **Post-go-live support**
CAPE Global Consulting provided post-go-live support. For the first month-end close, foreign currency valuation and translation was run for the first time using the new functionality in SAP General Ledger.

In April 2009 CMPC successfully reported consolidated financial statements by IFRS.

6.4   Key Findings

The key findings from the CMPC transition to IFRS can be summarized as follows:

▶ Start system changes such as upgrading to SAP ERP and migration to SAP General Ledger as soon as possible. These changes should run in parallel with the accounting changes.

▶ Identify the accounting differences between local GAAP and IFRS as early as possible. Sometimes, as for CMPC, legacy systems and interfaces need to be modified.

▶ Data clean-up before such a large migration is very important.

▶ A transition to IFRS requires a strong project manager.

▶ Having a trained project team and qualified consultants is essential.

▶ A significant amount of time is spent on testing.

6.5   Summary

This chapter provided a case study on a transition to IFRS for one of the largest companies in Chile. The project was completed on time and on budget and was a great success. At the time of writing, CMPC had reported IFRS financial statements for three quarters with very successful results. CMPC has also been live with SAP General Ledger for seven months without any problems and is using the parallel ledger functionality to report Chile local GAAP and tax.

Personally, I would like to thank the CMPC IFRS project team for their efforts in making this project so successful. These include the project manager, Eduardo Jure, his manager, Eduardo Sanchez, accounting Manager Alejandro Araya, and the team, including José Ramirez, Lisette Valero, Mary Jose Gonzalez Chandia, Abner Salinas, Pedro Gatica, Erick Burgos, and Jorge Venegas. I would also like to thank Chief Information Officer Alberto Compagnon for engaging CAPE Global Consulting on this project.

CAPE Global Consulting now has offices in Latin America, Canada, and the U.S. We specialize in assisting companies with their transition to IFRS and migrating to

SAP General Ledger as part of the IFRS transition. If you are considering a move to IFRS or a migration to SAP General Ledger, I can be contacted personally at *ptheobald@capeglobal.com*, and the company contact information is as follows:

CAPE Global Consulting Inc.

2850 Horizon Ridge Parkway Suite 200

Henderson, NV 89052, USA

+1 (702) 430-4774 (Office)

+1 (702) 430-4501 (Fax)

CAPE Global Consulting Latin America SpA

Avenida Vitacura 2939, Piso 10

Las Condes, Santiago, Chile

+56 2 431 53 15 (Office)

+56 2 431 50 50 (Fax)

CAPE Global Consulting Canada Ltd

10th Floor Bankers Hall, West Tower

#1000, 888 - 3rd St. SW

Calgary, Alberta

T2P 5C5, Canada

+1 (403) 444-6928 (Office)

+1 (403) 668-6001 (Fax)

Clients:	*sales@capeglobal.com*
Consultants:	*recruit@capeglobal.com*
General:	*info@capeglobal.com*

The Author

 **Paul Theobald**, CEO of CAPE Global Consulting Inc. (*www.CapeGlobal.com*), has worked with SAP since 1993. He has been an SAP ERP Financials consultant for 16 years and is also a qualified Chartered Accountant in the United Kingdom. Paul specializes in the SAP General Ledger and has consulted on several of the largest global SAP General Ledger migration projects. His company, CAPE Global Consulting, works actively with companies on the transition to IFRS and the SAP General Ledger migration that is often part of the larger IFRS project. He has worked on many major international SAP ERP Financials projects and has been lead consultant in various projects focused on the SAP General Ledger, Accounts Receivable, Accounts Payable, Banking, Fixed Assets, and the Special Ledger. Paul has lived and worked in the U.S. for 14 years and consulted for organizations around the world, making him uniquely qualified to understand the problems that arise in large, global implementations.

Index

Helps understand typical requirements for an SAP system audit

Proven insight on how auditors approach a system audit, and how to prepare an SAP system for successful audit

Roadmap of audit objectives for FI, CO, SD, BI/BW, MM, PP, and HR

Steve Biskie

Surviving an SAP Audit

This book is written to help SAP project managers, implementation teams, administrators, and users understand the typical audit requirements related to SAP. The book will give you practical, proven advice for preparing your specific domains for an internal or external SAP system audit by helping you learn to "think like an auditor" while preparing for an SAP audit.
It provides an overview of how auditors approach an SAP audit, discusses typical audit techniques. It covers specific SAP applications and components and their related business processes in detail.

approx. 510 pp., 89,95 Euro / US$ 89.95
ISBN 978-1-59229-253-0, Dec 2009

>> www.sap-press.com

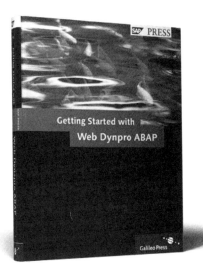

Covers all Finance-related processes, from purchasing and production to distribution

Teaches how to integrate Financial Accounting and Controlling with MM, PP, and SD

Details financial statement preparation and reporting

Andrea Hölzlwimmer

Optimizing Value Flows with SAP ERP

This book is written to teach financial consultants, IT managers, and integration consultants how value flows can be enhanced across an organization's entire finance and logistics chain. The book takes a process-oriented approach to the problems presented by non-integrated value flows in an organization and explains the solutions available in the SAP system. With this book you'll understand integrated value flows and learn about the important integration concepts, such as management of master data. You'll explore the central processes of purchasing, production, distribution accounting, and reporting, and you'll understand the impact of system settings and integration points as they relate to the overall process.

approx. 350 pp., 79,95 Euro / US$ 79.95
ISBN 978-1-59229-298-1,Dec 2009

>> www.sap-press.com

Provides a comprehensive guide to using the key SAP Geneeral Ledger functions effectively

Includes detailed coverage of SAP General Ledger processes, design, and customization options

Features extended sections on integration with subledgers, customization with BAPIs, and fast-close optimization

Shivesh Sharma

Maximizing SAP General Ledger

Successful integration of the SAP General Ledger into an existing infrastructure can make a significant impact on the ROI of an ERP Financials upgrade. Many users, however, lack the guidance necessary to sort through the integration and customization options available, particularly as consulting budgets are being slashed around the world. This book provides implementation teams, functional and technical teams, and end-users with a roadmap for the maximum utilization of the SAP General Ledger. This book focuses using the General Ledger in real-world situations and details how to customize and optimize it for specific business processes, and it teaches how to and integrate it with other SAP components. It will also help readers develop knowledge and strategies for enhancing the SAP General Ledger and integrating it with other SAP services and components.

approx. 500 pp., 79,95 Euro / US$ 79.95, ISBN 978-1-59229-306-3,Dec 2009

>> www.sap-press.com

Teaches how to design, configure, and implement the FSCM Collections, Dispute, Credit, and Biller Direct components

Provides proven guidance and real case studies for extending an ERP Financials infrastructure with FSCM

Includes coverage of advanced topics including extensions, reporting with NetWeaver BI, and workflow design

Sreedhar Narahari

Receivables and Collections Automation with SAP FSCM

The primary purpose of the book is to provide finance team members, implementation project managers, and consultants with a comprehensive, practical guide to the FSCM applications available for automating the receivables and collections management functions. Focusing primarily on the core functions of the Biller Direct, Credit Management, Collections Management, and Dispute Management applications, the book offers readers a roadmap for implementation, integration, and customization.

approx. 450 pp., 79,95 Euro / US$ 79.95
ISBN 978-1-59229-245-5, March 2010

>> www.sap-press.com

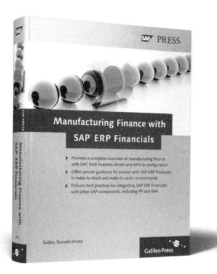

Provides a complete overview of manufacturing finance with SAP, from business drivers and KPIs to configuration and integration

Offers proven guidance for success with SAP ERP Financials in make-to-stock and make-to-order manufacturing environments

Subbu Ramakrishnan

Manufacturing Finance with SAP ERP Financials

The primary purpose of the book is to provide finance team members, implementation project managers, and consultants with a comprehensive, practical guide to the Finance functionality available for the manufacturing environment and the configuration and integration processes necessary for optimizing ERP Financials for manufacturing. Focusing primarily on the core functions of the Financial Accounting and Controlling components, the book provides readers with a holistic look at the business drivers, KPIs, configuration schemes, and technical issues relevant to the manufacturing finance function. It presents a solution-oriented view of manufacturing finance that includes the integration of ERP Financials components with other SAP applications critical to the manufacturing operation, such as Production Planning and Materials Management.

580 pp., 2009, 79,95 Euro / US$ 79.95, ISBN 978-1-59229-238-7

>> www.sap-press.com

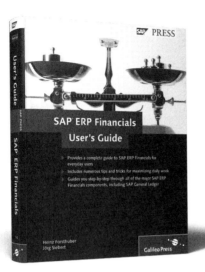

Get to know how to use SAP
Financials in your daily work

Learn step by step how to master the
processes of financial accounting

Up-to-date for SAP ERP 6.0

Heinz Forsthuber, Jörg Siebert

SAP ERP Financials User's Guide

This easy-to-read book will cover all the functionality of SAP ERP
Financials. It will be custom-tailored for users in the Finance and
Accounting departments. Readers will learn how to best use SAP ERP
Financials in their daily work. Using step-by-step descriptions, practical
examples and many figures, it will be easy to follow even for those new
to ERP Financials. The robust appendices help readers provide readers
with additional information: an introduction to the SAP system,
transaction and menu paths, a glossary and two indices. The book is
based on SAP ERP 6.0.

593 pp., 2009, 69,95 Euro / US$ 69.95
ISBN 978-1-59229-190-8

>> www.sap-press.com

Interested in reading more?

Please visit our Web site for all
new book releases from SAP PRESS.

www.sap-press.com